CLARENCE L. AND ESTHER S. MEYERS LIBRARY
Reform Congregation Keneseth Israel
Elkins Park 17, Pa.

Anti-Semitism in Europe:

Sources of the Holocaust

Anti-Semitism in Europe:

Sources of the Holocaust

Edited by DAVID W. ZISENWINE
Introduction by ROBERT CHAZAN

*THE JEWISH CONCEPTS
AND ISSUES SERIES*

Series Editor: SEYMOUR ROSSEL

BEHRMAN HOUSE, INC. NEW YORK, N.Y. 10001

ACKNOWLEDGMENTS

The editor and publisher thank the following for permission to reprint:
American Zionist Youth Foundation for selection from *The Holocaust* edited by Muki Tzur and Nathan Yanai, by American Zionist Youth Foundation. L. B. Fischer for selection from *Warsaw Ghetto: A Diary* by Mary Berg, edited by S. L. Shneiderman © 1945 by L. B. Fischer. Hans Habe for selection from *The Mission* published by Coward-McCann, Inc. © 1966 by Hans Habe. Hebrew Union College Press for selection from *Concerning the Amelioration of the Civil Status of the Jews* by Christian Wilhelm Dohm © 1957 by Ellis Rivkin. Holt, Rinehart, and Winston, Publishers for selection from *The Holocaust Kingdom: A Memoir* by Alexander Donat © 1963, 1965 by Alexander Donat. Houghton Mifflin Company for selection from *Mein Kampf* by Adolf Hitler, translated by Ralph Manheim © 1943 by Houghton Mifflin Company. Jewish Publication Society of America for selection from *Anthology of Holocaust Literature* edited by Jacob Glatstein, Israel Knox, Samuel Margoshes © 1968 by Jewish Publication Society of America. McGraw-Hill Book Company for selection from *Notes From the Warsaw Ghetto: The Journal of Emmanuel Ringelblum* edited by Jacob Sloan © 1958 by Jacob Sloan. McGraw-Hill Book Company for selection from *The Murderers Among Us: The Wiesenthal Memoirs* edited by Joseph Wechsberg © 1967 by Opera Mundi, Paris. Donia Rosen for selection from *The Forest, My Friend* published by Bergen-Belsen Memorial Press © 1971 by Donia Rosen.

Library of Congress Cataloging in Publication Data

Main entry under title:

Anti-Semitism in Europe.

(The Jewish concepts and issues series)
SUMMARY: A collection of primary sources tracing the development of anti-Semitism in Europe from the seventeenth century to the Nazi period.
1. Holocaust, Jewish (1939-1945)–Addresses, essays, lectures. 2. Antisemitism–History–Sources. [1. Holocaust, Jewish (1939-1945)–Addresses, essays, lectures. 2. Antisemitism–History–Sources] I. Zisenwine, David W.
D810.J4A63   940.53'1503'924   76-47452
ISBN O-87441-228-5

© Copyright 1976 by David W. Zisenwine

Published by Behrman House, Inc.

1261 Broadway, New York, N.Y. 10001

CONTENTS

INTRODUCTION by Robert Chazan   vii

PREFACE   ix

ONE: Emancipation: Demands and Opportunities   1

TWO: **Late Nineteenth-Century Achievement:**   11
Alfred Dreyfus
A Sketch of My Life

THREE: **Late Nineteenth-Century Failure:**   14
Alfred Dreyfus
*The Degradation: A Hostile
Newspaper Account*

FOUR: **Hitler's Anti-Semitism**   18
Speech of July 28, 1922, in Munich
Speech of September 18, 1922, in Munich
Racial Theory and Planning (from *Mein Kampf*)
Adolf Hitler's Anti-Semitism (from *Mein Kampf*)

FIVE: **Nazi Legislation**   30
*Law for the Protection of the
German Blood and the German Honor*
The Reich Citizenship Law

SIX: **Unwanted!**   35
The Refugees

SEVEN: **Murder**   39
Testimony from the Nuremberg Trials

EIGHT:	**Isolation** 43	
	Emmanuel Ringelblum	
	Mary Berg	
NINE:	**The Roundup** 56	
TEN:	**Systematic Destruction** 61	
	Technological Destruction	
	Testimony from the Nuremberg Trials	
ELEVEN:	**Jewish Resistance** 67	
	Warsaw Ghetto Revolt	
	A Manifesto: Jewish Resistance in Vilna	
	Mordecai Anilewicz's Last Letter	
TWELVE:	**War Trials** 72	
	Executive Order by President Truman:	
	May 2, 1945	
	Agreement: August 8, 1945	
	Charter: August 8, 1945	
	Report to the President by	
	Mr. Justice Jackson: October 7, 1946	
	Testimony from the Nuremberg Trials	
	Eichmann, The Elusive	
THIRTEEN:	**Feelings** 85	
	"The Lonely Child"	
	"A Jewish Child"	
	"Twilight in the Children's Sick Room"	
	"The Grabber's Prayer"	
	Memoirs of Humanity	

FOR FURTHER READING   97
A GUIDE FOR DISCUSSION   99

INTRODUCTION

The past two centuries have seen cataclysmic change in the Jewish world. Major restructuring of the general political and economic order has meant for the Jews exhilarating new opportunities and unspeakable tragedies. Awareness of these tumultuous developments is obviously critical for an understanding of the past and present condition of the Jews. Indeed, the student of modern western history has much to learn from the Jewish experience, for many of the most significant achievements and failures of modern, western society express themselves dramatically in the saga of the Jews.

Approximately two years ago a small group of scholars and educators began to investigate methods for making this stormy chapter in Jewish history better understood and more deeply felt in the setting of both Jewish and non-Jewish schools. The basic technique adopted was the utilization of brief and significant source selections. The assumption was that, if useful source selections could be isolated, students would be challenged to reconstruct for themselves crucial developments in modern Jewish history. In addition to the intellectual stimulation, source selections present the student with some of the passion and pathos of the life experience of individual men and women; they transform the study of history from the abstract to the real.

The collection of sources presented here represents the first achievement of this program. These materials have been tested and retested in Jewish and general school courses at various levels. After each utilization of the sources, there has been an extensive evaluation, drawing on the reactions of students, teachers, and outside observers. It is our hope that this volume and its successors will afford its readers as much insight and understanding as it has afforded those of us who have participated in the two years of the pilot project.

ROBERT CHAZAN

PREFACE

A proper study of any historical period or event must deal with the interpretation of a great variety of information. The purpose of this book of source material is to allow you to read what the participants in this drama felt was happening to them and to the culture in which they lived. The primary sources are taken from speeches, diaries, newspapers, memoirs, and government documents. Reading them opens the possibility for further analysis and interpretation. It allows you to enter the historical process, if only for a brief moment, to gain your own sense of a complicated period in Jewish history.

The readings are not confined to the period of the Holocaust itself, but reach back to the days of emancipation and continue through the post-war trials to offer a more comprehensive view of the antecedents, as well as the aftermath, of this tragic moment in world history. This reader offers one possible method of approaching history. It is the editor's hope that the selections will lead you to further research, investigation, and analysis.

To my father and the memory of my mother

ONE

Emancipation: Demands and Opportunities

Prior to modern times the Jewish communities of the world were generally scattered, small, and weak. Jews were separated from Christian neighbors, and the Jewish community often formed a city within a city, a ghetto. Jews were subject to special taxes. They were forced to develop and run separate school systems, as well as separate Jewish welfare institutions. Thus, the pre-modern Jewish community had very little contact with the surrounding majority culture. In general, prior to the seventeenth century, a ruling class of lords or nobles controlled minority cultures and groups. Both ruler and ruled saw this arrangement as a given reality, one that had to be recognized and accepted. Rules were not always harmful to the Jews. For example, Jews in early seventeenth-century Holland lived under a very generous regime, but the arbitrary nature of rules and rulers was still a fact of Jewish life.

By the eighteenth century it was obvious that a change was coming. The old social order had begun to break down. The Roman Catholic Church had been the central institution dictating the nature of the society, but with the onset of the Protestant reformation and a series of costly wars, a restructuring of society began. In very general terms, the state became the institution which dealt with the material aspects of society, and the church became part of the private sphere.

This separation of Church and State led to the question of just what should be the place of the Jew in this new social order. Churchmen and statesmen differed in their opinions on the nature of Jews and Judaism. One group saw the Jews as hopelessly separate from Christian society, whether Catholic or Protestant. They considered the Jews unproductive economic entities at best, and a parasitic money-lending, peddler class, at worst. They also viewed the Jews as uncultured and totally incapable of being equal participants in a Christian state.

A second group, the liberals, also saw the Jews as a downtrodden element, but said that the conditions of the old social order had led to their wretched state. They felt that, given the proper conditions, the Jews could be useful and productive citizens. This notion that Jews were a victim of the environment implied that there were no racial or inherent characteristics of the Jews which had led to their miserable condition in society.

One of the most articulate spokesmen for this liberal group was Christian Wilhelm Dohm (1751-1820), an enlightened Prussian statesman who, in 1781, published his views in a work entitled *Concerning The Amelioration of the Civil Status of the Jews*. Dohm's essay became a model for broad-minded arguments in the exciting 1780's and 90's in France. Here is an excerpt from it:

> The Jews of each state are already more at home there than strangers can become in a long time. They know no other fatherland than the one given to them now and do not long for a far-away homeland. They are not uncivilized and savage gypsies, nor ignorant and unmannerly refugees. Many of them in every state have the same property, and many more have excellent gifts of intellect and skill. If it is permissible to draw conclusions from the

majority of a nation about its essential qualities, no one can deny that the Jews possess excellent intelligence, industry, and the capability to adjust to all kinds of situations. If Jews are made use of in public business, one is almost always very satisfied with their zeal and sagacity. Their luck in commerce and manufacture is well known, and often those who envy them ascribe to fraud what is only a consequence of their greater industry and application. Where they are allowed to be artisans and workers, they usually do excellent work. The oppression under which they have lived until now is at fault if they have not done more in the sciences and fine arts; they certainly do not lack the capability. Most of those who occupied themselves with these interests have made good progress, even if they are not known to the public like a Moses Mendelssohn and a Pinto. Among their greater merchants one finds perhaps more broad view and skill in coordination, and among their common people, more intelligence and industry than among an equal number of Christians. As regards the moral character of the Jews, it is like that of all men: capable of the most lofty development and of the most unfortunate deterioration, and as I remarked already, the influence of the external environment is quite clearly visible. If one admits, however, that Jews are in certain points morally corrupt, the impartial observer has to admit that their fine traits show even greater excellence in other points. I dare to count as a fine trait of the Jewish character the steadfast adherence to the Law given to their fathers by the Deity himself, and I hope to have in this, the agreement of all who do not demand that they should share with them the belief of their childhood, and who are not so hampered by the prejudices of their upbringing that they cannot be just toward these same prejudices in others. What seems clear and undeniable to the Christian looks dark and contradictory to the Jew; what the Christian calls blindness and stiff-necked stubbornness to the Jew is steadfast adherence to what he believes to be a divine Law. And if we want to be impartial, can we blame him if he remains for so long steadfast and faithful to the truth as he sees it, until he finds the happiness to be convinced of a better truth, a happiness which according to the unanimous teachings of Christians and philosophers nobody can bring about by himself, and which according to Christian teaching is portioned out from above? The faithful adherence to principles one holds to be true is the measure of a man's moral worth, and who can deny honor to the Jew, whom no torture can make eat what he thinks God himself has forbidden him, and who despises the low renegade, who for financial profit tears himself away from the holy faith of his youth, from his relatives and from his people, and who debases the holy faith of the Christians by professing it without being convinced of its divine truth.

This adherence to the ancient faith of their fathers alone gives the character of the Jews a firmness, which is also very advantageous for the formation of their general morality. The strict observation of many burdensome commandments and customs nourishes, it is true, a certain pettiness, makes them set too much store in the observation of ceremonies, but on the other hand it keeps them from many misdeeds, and in general prepares them for a more precise fulfillment of their duties.

A very happy influence on the moral character of the Jews has been their closeness and segregation, forced on them in part by their strange religion, and in part by oppression. Their almost equal fate has linked all Jews so closely with one another that they share in the fate of their fellow-Jews with much more interest than is possible in a more numerous nation. Nowhere are their poor a burden on the state; they are taken care of by the prosperous among them and the whole community takes sympathetic interest in the affairs of the individual. The Jews seem to enjoy the bliss of domestic life with more simplicity than is at present usual, at least in big cities. Most of them are good husbands and fathers. Luxury has with them not yet reached the stage as with Christians in similar circumstances. The purity of their marriages is greater, crimes of unchastity, especially perversities, are much rarer. Almost never has a Jew committed treachery or a crime against the state. Almost everywhere they are devoted to the country in which they live, if only they are not treated too badly. In danger they have shown a zeal which one would not have expected from members of society who are so little favored.

If this reasoning is correct, then we have found in the

oppression and in the restricted occupation of the Jews the true source of their corruption. Then we have discovered also at the same time the means of healing this corruption and of making the Jews better men and useful citizens. With the elimination of the unjust and unpolitical treatment of the Jews will also disappear the consequences of it; and when we cease to limit them to one kind of occupation, then the detrimental influence of that occupation will no longer be noticeable. With the modesty that a private citizen should always show when expressing his thoughts about public affairs, and with the certain conviction that general proposals should always be tailored, if they should be useful, to the special local conditions in every state, I dare now, after these remarks, to submit my ideas as to the manner in which the Jews could become happier and better members of civil societies.

To make them such it is *first* necessary to give them equal rights with all other subjects. Since they are able to fulfill the necessary duties, they should be allowed to claim the equal impartial love and care of the state. No humiliating discrimination should be tolerated, no way of earning a living should be closed to them, none other than the regular taxes demanded from them. They would have to pay all the usual taxes in the state, but they would not have to pay protection money for the mere right to exist, no special fee for the permission to earn a living. It is obvious that in accordance with the principle of equal rights, also special privileges favoring the Jews—which exist in some states—would have to be abolished . . .

Second, since it is primarily the limitation of the Jews to commerce which has had a detrimental influence on their moral and political character, a perfect freedom in the choice of a livelihood would serve justice, as well as represent a humanitarian policy which would make the Jews more useful and happier members of society.

It might even be useful, in order to achieve this great purpose, if the government would first try to dissuade the Jews from the occupation of commerce, and endeavor to weaken its influence by encouraging them to prefer such kinds of livelihoods as are most apt to create a diametrically opposed spirit and character—I mean artisan occupations . . .

Third, the Jews should not be excluded from agriculture. Unless the purchase of landed property is restricted in a country to certain classes of the inhabitants, the Jews should not be excluded, and they should have equal rights to lease land . . .

Fourth, no kind of commerce should be closed to the Jews, but none should be left to them exclusively, nor should they be encouraged by privileges . . .

Fifth, every art, every science should be open to the Jew as to every other free man. He, too, should educate his mind as far as he is able; he, too, must be able to rise to promotion, honor, and rewards by developing his talents. The scientific institutions of the state should be for his use, too, and he should be as free as other citizens to utilize his talents in any way.

Sixth, it should be a special endeavor of a wise government to care for the moral education and enlightenment of the Jews, in order to make at least the coming generations more receptive to a milder treatment and the enjoyment of all advantages of our society . . .

Seventh, with the moral improvement of the Jews there should go hand in hand efforts of the Christians to get rid of their prejudices and uncharitable opinions. In early childhood they should be taught to regard the Jews as their brothers and fellowmen who seek to find favor with God in a different way—a way they think erroneously to be the right one, yet which, if they follow in sincerity of heart, God looks at with favor . . .

(From Christian Wilhelm Dohm, *Concerning the Amelioration of the Civil Status of the Jews)*

By the end of the eighteenth century, the Jews seemed ready to accept the new definitions of their status presented by men such as Dohm, and appeared eager to become part of this changing order. However, the new opportunities were not without their demands and an accompanying persistent suspicion of the Jewish community. The enlightened Christians expected change and the Jewish community had to work out its relationship carefully to these demands.

The French Revolution [1789] led to lofty statements about equality, but the details of the meaning of that equality were left to the National Assembly which met from August, 1789, to September, 1791. One of the last issues raised in the closing moments of debate was the status of the Jews, and only after heated discussion and the appeal to the need for consistency were the Jews given full civil rights in France.

However, the suspicion about Jewish loyalty was difficult to uproot, so Napoleon summoned a group of "Jewish notables," rabbis, and distinguished communal leaders, to answer what he felt were basic questions. The following selection, reporting on the proceedings of the Assembly of Notables, which met from July 30 to August 12, 1806, illustrates in a most dramatic way the difficulties that the Jewish community had to face.

Gentlemen:
His Majesty, the Emperor and King, having named us Commissioners to transact whatever relates to you, has this day sent us to this assembly to acquaint you with his intentions. Called together from the extremities of this vast empire, no one among you is ignorant of the object for which His Majesty has convened this assembly. You know it. The conduct of many among those of your persuasion has excited complaints, which have found their way to the foot of the throne; these complaints were founded on truth. Nevertheless, His Majesty has been satisfied with stopping the progress of the evil, and he has wished to hear you on the means of providing a remedy. You will, no doubt, prove worthy of so tender, so paternal a conduct, and you will feel all the importance of the truth thus reposed in you. Far from considering the government under which you live as a power against which you should be on your guard, you will assist it with your experience and cooperate with it in all the good it intends; thus you will prove that, following the example of all Frenchmen, you do not seclude yourselves from the rest of mankind.

The laws which have been imposed on individuals of your religion have been different in the several parts of the world: often they have been dictated by the interest of the day. But as an assembly like the present has no precedent in the annals of Christianity, so will you be judged, for the first time, with justice, and you will see your fate irrevocably fixed by a Christian Prince. The wish of His Majesty is that you should be Frenchmen; it remains with you to accept the proffered title, without forgetting that, to prove unworthy of it, would be renouncing it altogether.

You will hear the questions submitted to you: your duty is to answer the whole truth on every one of them. Attend, and never lose sight of that which we are going to tell you; that, when a monarch equally firm and just, who knows everything, and who punishes or recompenses every action, puts questions to his subjects, these would be equally guilty and blind to their true interests, if they were to disguise the truth in the least.

The intention of His Majesty is, Gentlemen, that you should enjoy the greatest freedom in your deliberations; your answers will be transmitted to us by your President, when they have been put in regular form.

As to us, our most ardent wish is to be able to report to the Emperor that, among individuals of the Jewish persuasion, he can reckon as many faithful subjects, determined to conform in everything to the laws and to the morality which ought to regulate the conduct of all Frenchmen.

One of the Secretaries then read the following twelve questions proposed by the Commissioners:

Questions proposed to Assembly of the Jews by the Commissioners named by his Majesty the Emperor and King to transact whatever concerns them.

1. Is it lawful for Jews to marry more than one wife?
2. Is divorce allowed by the Jewish religion? Is divorce valid, although not pronounced by courts of justice and by virtue of laws in contradiction with the French Code?
3. Can a Jewess marry a Christian, or a Jew a Christian woman? Or has the law ordered that the Jews should only intermarry among themselves?
4. In the eyes of Jews are Frenchmen considered as brethren or as strangers?
5. In either case, what conduct does their law prescribe toward Frenchmen not of their religion?
6. Do the Jews born in France, and treated by the law as

French citizens, acknowledge France as their country? Are they bound to defend it? Are they bound to obey the laws, and to follow the directions of the civil code?
7. What kind of police jurisdiction have the rabbis among the Jews? What judicial power do they exercise among them?
8. Are the forms of the elections of the rabbis and their police jurisdiction regulated by the law, or are they only sanctioned by custom?
9. Are there professions from which the Jews are excluded by their law?
10. Does the law forbid the Jews from taking usury from their brethren?
11. Does it forbid or does it allow usury toward strangers?

During the reading of these questions, the assembly manifested by unanimous and spontaneous emotions how deeply it was affected by the doubt which the questions seemed to convey, as to the attachment of Frenchmen, following the law of Moses, for their fellow citizens, and for their country, and as to their sense of the duty by which they are bound to defend it.

The assembly was not able to conceal the emotions caused by the sixth question, in which it is asked if Jews born in France and treated by the law as French citizens acknowledge France as their country and if they are bound to defend it. The whole assembly unanimously exclaimed, "Even to death" . . .

(From Diogene Tama, ed., *Transactions of the Parisian Sanhedrin or Acts of the Assembly of Israelitish Deputies of France and Italy,* translated by F. D. Kirwan)

From the insulting first question to the more complex challenge of Jewish loyalty to French society, the questions certainly reveal the nature and extent of the doubts which existed. The Notables responded as best they could, but their answers were regarded as inadequate. A larger body, therefore, the Great Sanhedrin, was called into session to deal with these issues.

Napoleon ultimately resolved in favor of equal rights for Jews, but the feeling of uneasiness, and the need on their part, to prove their loyalty and devotion to the state became a constant theme in nineteenth century Jewish life. Jews moved out into French society, and participated with zeal and loyalty, but the residual doubts never vanished.

NINETEENTH-CENTURY ACHIEVEMENT

April 21, I was married. I left the Ecole Superieure de Guerre in 1892 with the degree "very good," and the brevet of Staff Officer. My rank number on leaving the Ecole entitled me to be detailed as *stagiaire* [probationer] on the General Staff of the army. I took service in the Second Bureau of the General Staff [The Intelligence Bureau] on the 1st of January, 1893.

A brilliant and easy career was opened to me; the future appeared under the most promising auspices. After my day's work I found rest and delight at home. Every manifestation of the human mind was of profound interest to me. I found pleasure in reading aloud during the long evenings passed at my wife's side. We were perfectly happy, and our first child, a boy, brightened our home; I had no material cares, and the same deep affection united me to the family of my wife as the members of my own family. Everything in life seemed to smile on me.

(From Alfred Dreyfus, *Five Years of My Life*)

TWO

Late Nineteenth-Century Achievement: Alfred Dreyfus

Time passed. The issues raised by Napoleon seemed to have faded and the emancipation of the Jews seemed totally assured. In much of Europe, Jews no longer lived in ghettos, nor did they speak a strange language or wear strange clothes. They were no longer restricted in business or professional life. The Jews were no longer seen as just a religious group. They had entered into the mainstream of European life.

In earlier days, when prejudice threatened, the only exit for a Jew was religious conversion. Now, the haters and bigots rephrased their hatred in racial or national terms. The old doubts may have shed one skin, but the snake was the same. Since to be "anti-Jewish" on religious grounds was no longer appropriate, there emerged a new way of seeing the Jew in modern terms as an alien race or as foreign nationals. "Anti-Semitism," not anti-Judaism, became the label of the late-nineteenth century's accommodation to the changes in social structure and status of the Jewish community.

The Dreyfus case illustrates how this new attitude worked. It was not the first manifestation of anti-Semitism nor was it the last. But it was a landmark case which rocked late-nineteenth-century French society, was a source of fervent public debate, and eventually even contributed to the fall of several French governments.

Alfred Dreyfus, a French Jew, saw himself as a Frenchman, precisely as Dohm and Napoleon had hoped. He had become a Captain in the French army, when suddenly he was falsely accused of treason, of selling military secrets to the Germans. The following selection from his diary, *Five Years of My Life,* illustrates Dreyfus' feeling of success and his total integration into French society.

A Sketch of My Life

I was born at Mulhouse, in Alsace, October 9, 1859. My childhood passed happily amid the gentle influences of mother and sisters, a kind father devoted to his children, and the companionship of older brothers.

My first sorrow was the Franco-Prussian War. It has never faded from my memory. When peace was concluded my father chose the French nationality, and we had to leave Alsace. I went to Paris to continue my studies.

In 1878 I was received at the Ecole Polytechnique, which in the usual order of things I left in 1880, to enter, as cadet of artillery, the Ecole d'Application of Fontainebleau, where I spent the regulation two years. After graduating, on the 1st of October, 1882, I was breveted lieutenant in the Thirty-first Regiment of Artillery in the garrison at Le Mans. At the end of the year 1883, I was transferred to the Horse Batteries of the First Independent Cavalry Division, at Paris. On the 12th of September, 1889, I received my commission of captain in the Twenty-First Regiment of Artillery, and was appointed on special service at the Ecole Centrale de Pyrotechnie Militaire at Bourges. It was in the course of the following winter that I became engaged to Mlle. Lucie Hadamard, my devoted and heroic wife.

During my engagement I prepared myself for the Ecole Superieure de Guerre [School for Staff Officers], where I was received the 20th of April, 1890; the next day,

April 21, I was married. I left the Ecole Superieure de Guerre in 1892 with the degree "very good," and the brevet of Staff Officer. My rank number on leaving the Ecole entitled me to be detailed as *stagiaire* [probationer] on the General Staff of the army. I took service in the Second Bureau of the General Staff [The Intelligence Bureau] on the 1st of January, 1893.

A brilliant and easy career was opened to me; the future appeared under the most promising auspices. After my day's work I found rest and delight at home. Every manifestation of the human mind was of profound interest to me. I found pleasure in reading aloud during the long evenings passed at my wife's side. We were perfectly happy, and our first child, a boy, brightened our home; I had no material cares, and the same deep affection united me to the family of my wife as the members of my own family. Everything in life seemed to smile on me.

(From Alfred Dreyfus, *Five Years of My Life*)

THREE

Late Nineteenth-Century Failure: Alfred Dreyfus

Dreyfus' feeling of accomplishment and success were soon shattered. The charge of treason, based, to some extent, on Dreyfus' Jewish origins, demonstrated the failure of the French Jews' hopes of emancipation. Dreyfus was publicly degraded on Saturday, January 5th, 1894. One French newspaper reported the scene as follows:

> *The Degradation:*
> *A Hostile Newspaper Account*
>
> The first stroke of nine sounds from the school clock. General Darras lifts his sword and gives the command, which is repeated at the head of each company: 'Portez armes!'
>
> The troops obey.
>
> A complete silence ensues.
>
> Hearts stop beating, and all eyes are turned toward the corner of the vast square, where Dreyfus has been shut up in a small building.
>
> Soon a little group appears: it is Alfred Dreyfus who is advancing, between four artillerymen, accompanied by a Lieutenant of the Republican Guard and the oldest

non-commissioned officer of the regiment. Between the dark dolmans of the gunners we see distinctly the gold of the three stripes and the gold of the capbands; the sword glitters, and even at this distance we behold the black sword-knot on the hilt of the sword.

Dreyfus marches with a steady step.

"Look, see how straight the wretch is carrying himself," someone says.

The group advances toward General Darras, with whom is the clerk of the Court Martial, M. Vallecale.

There are cries now in the crowd.

But the group halts.

A sign from the officer in command, the drums beat, and the trumpets blow, and then again all is still; a tragic silence now.

The artillerymen with Dreyfus drop back a few steps, and the condemned man stands well out in full view of us all.

The clerk salutes the General, and turning towards Dreyfus reads distinctly the verdict: "The said Dreyfus is condemned to military degradation and to deportation to a fortress."

The clerk turns to the General and salutes. Dreyfus has listened in silence. The voice of General Darras is then heard, and although it is slightly tremulous with emotion, we catch distinctly this phrase:

"Dreyfus, you are unworthy to wear the uniform. In the name of the French people, we deprive you of your rank."

Thereupon we behold Dreyfus lift his arms in air, and, his head well up, exclaim in a loud voice, in which there is not the slightest tremor:

"I am innocent. I swear that I am innocent. Vive la France!"

In reply the immense throng without clamors, "Death to the traitor!"

But the noise is instantly hushed. Already the adjutant whose melancholy duty it is to strip from the prisoner his stripes and arms has begun his work, and they now begin to strew the ground.

Dreyfus makes this the occasion of a fresh protest, and his cries carry distinctly even to the crowd outside:

"In the name of my wife and children, I swear that I am innocent. I swear it. Vive la France!"

But the work has been rapid. The adjutant has torn quickly the stripes from the hat, the embroideries from the cuffs, the buttons from the dolman, the numbers from the collar, and ripped off the red stripe worn by the prisoner ever since his entrance into the Polytechnic School.

The sabre remains: the adjutant draws it from its scabbard and breaks it across his knee. There is a dry click, and the two portions are flung with the insignia upon the ground. Then the belt is detached, and in its turn the scabbard falls.

This is the end. These few seconds have seemed to us ages. Never was there a more terrible sensation of anguish.

And once more, clear and passionless, comes the voice of the prisoner:

"You are degrading an innocent man."

He must now pass along the line in front of his former comrades and subordinates. For another the torture would have been horrible. Dreyfus does not seem to be affected, however, for he leaps over the insignia of his rank, which two gendarmes are shortly to gather up, and takes his place between the four gunners, who, with drawn swords, have led him before General Darras.

The little group, led by two officers of the Republican Guard, moves toward the band of music in front of the prison van and begins its march along the front of the troops and about three feet distant from them.

Dreyfus holds his head well up. The public cries, "Death to the traitor!" Soon he reaches the great gateway, and the crowd has a better sight of him. The cries increase, thousands of voices demanding the death of the wretch, who still exclaims: "I am innocent! Vive la France!"

The crowd has not heard, but it has seen Dreyfus turn toward it and speak.

A formidable burst of hisses replies to him, then an immense shout which rolls like a tempest across the vast courtyard:

"Death to the traitor! Kill him!"

And then, outside, the mob heaves forward in a murderous surge. Only by a mighty effort can the police restrain the people from breaking through into the yard, to wreak their swift and just vengeance upon Dreyfus for his infamy.

Dreyfus continues his march. He reaches the group made up of the press representatives.

"You will say to the whole of France," he cries, "that I am innocent!"

"Silence, wretch," is the reply. "Coward! Traitor! Judas!"

Under the insult, the abject Dreyfus pulls himself up. He flings at us a glance full of fierce hatred.

"You have no right to insult me!"

A clear voice issues from the group:

"You know well that you are not innocent. Vive la France! Dirty Jew!"

Dreyfus continues his route.

His clothing is pitiably disheveled. In the place of his stripes hang long dangling threads, and his cap has no shape.

Dreyfus pulls himself up once more, but the cries of the crowd are beginning to affect him. Though the head of the wretch is still insolently turned toward the troops, his legs are beginning to give way.

The march round the square is ended. Dreyfus is handed over to the two gendarmes, who have gathered up his stripes, and they conduct him to the prison van.

... Dreyfus, completely silent now, is placed once more in prison. But there again he protests his innocence.

(From Alfred Dreyfus, *Five Years of My Life*)

FOUR

Hitler's Anti-Semitism

Following their defeats in the Napoleonic wars, the fragmented German states were in total disarray. Slowly, they began their search for national identity and integrity, but in this quest they rejected the Enlightenment and its ideal of the perfectability of all men. The German striving for national integrity always excluded the idea of the Jew entering normative German society. The Jew was an outsider and the new Germany excluded him. The nineteenth century, thus, had periods of reaction and anti-Semitism mixed with periods of liberalism and the growth of a commitment to civil rights for all men.

In this turbulence the foundation was laid for the ideas which were to engulf all of Germany.

The frustration and bitterness of German defeat in World War I led to a forceful resurgence of nationalism and a further rejection of the liberalism of the French Revolution. Political parties were founded which had, as their platforms, nationalism and the restoration of German pride. The Nazi party (National Socialist German Workers' Party) was one of these.

The old promise of emancipation, and of a new social

order in which the Jew could realize his potential as a full citizen in an open society were soon to be challenged and destroyed. The progress of the past was soon to be obliterated with the rise of Hitler in Nazi Germany.

Adolf Hitler, born in Linz, Austria, migrated to Vienna and then to Munich, Germany, in 1913. He enlisted in the German army in 1914 and joined the Nazi party after the war.

Hitler emerged as the most articulate spokesman for his party's program, and began to formulate a platform of action for party leadership. In his early speeches it is possible to see the evolution of his anti-Semitism, and the embryonic stages of his ultimate goal of the total destruction of the Jewish people.

The following section is taken from some of those early speeches. The style is neither eloquent nor sophisticated, but it was appealing to a country in quest of its honor. These speeches vividly illustrate the intentions of Adolf Hitler. In this first speech Hitler speaks directly to the issue of emancipation and the Jews:

> ... It is a battle which began nearly 120 years ago, at the moment when the Jew was granted citizen rights in the European States. The political emancipation of the Jews was the beginning of an attack of delirium. For thereby there were given full citizen rights and equality to a people which was much more clearly and definitely a race apart than all others, that has always formed and will form a State within the State. That did not happen perhaps at one blow, but it came about as things come about today and always do come about: first a little finger, then a second and a third, and so bit by bit until at last a people that in the eighteenth century still appeared completely alien had won equal citizen rights with ourselves.
>
> And it was precisely the same in the economic sphere. The vast process of the industrialization of the peoples meant the confluence of great masses of workmen in the towns. Thus great hordes of people arose, and these, more's the pity, were not properly dealt with by those whose moral duty it was to concern themselves for their

welfare. Parallel with this was a gradual "moneyfication" of the whole of the nation's labor-strength. "Share-capital" was in the ascendant, and thus bit by bit the Stock Exchange came to control the whole national economy. The directors of these institutions were, and are without exception, Jews. I say "without exception," for the few non-Jews who had a share in them are in the last resort nothing but screens, shop-window Christians, whom one needs in order, for the sake of the masses, to keep up the appearance that these institutions were after all founded as a natural outcome of the needs and the economic life of all peoples alike, and were not, as was the fact, institutions which correspond only with the essential characteristics of the Jewish people and are the outcome of those characteristics....

... In consequence of this widespread aversion it was more difficult for the Jew to spread infection in the political sphere, and especially so since traditionally loyalty was centered in a person: the form of the State was a monarchy, and power did not lie with an irresponsible majority. Thus the Jew saw that here it was possible for an enlightened despotism to arise based upon the army, the bureaucracy, and the masses of the people still unaffected by the Jewish poison. The intelligentsia at that time was almost exclusively German, big business and the new industries were in German hands, while the last reservoir of a people's strength, the peasantry, was throughout healthy. In such conditions if, as industry grew, a fourth estate was formed in the towns, there was the danger that this fourth estate might ally itself with the monarchy, and thus with its support there might arise a popular monarchy (*Volkskönig*) or a popular *Kaisertum* which would be ready and willing to give a mortal blow to those powers of international supra-State finance which were at that time beginning to grow in influence. This was not impossible: in the history of Germany princes had from time to time found themselves forced, as in Brandenburg, to turn against the nobility and seek popular support ...

But this possibility constituted a grave danger for Jewry. If the great masses of the new industrialized workmen had come into Nationalist hands and like a true social leaven had penetrated the whole nation, if the liberation of the different estates (*Stände*) had followed step by step in an organic development and the State had later looked to them for support, then there would have been created what many hoped for in November, 1918, viz., a national social State. For Socialism in itself is anything but an international creation. As a noble conception it has indeed grown up exclusively in Aryan hearts; it owes its intellectual glories only to Aryan brains. It is entirely alien to the Jew.

(From Adolf Hitler, *My New Order*. Speech of July 28, 1922, in Munich)

Hitler linked the frustrations of the German defeat in World War I, and the resurgence of German national pride to the presence of Jews. He was direct and explicit in his goals. His speech in Munich on September 18, 1922, was unequivocal in its conviction that Jews had no place in German society, and that they must be expelled from the country. In these early stages he had not yet arrived at his final solution—genocide!

... Economics is a secondary matter. World history teaches us that no people became great through economics: it was economics that brought them to their ruin. A people died when its race was disintegrated. Germany, too, did not become great through economics.

A people that in its own life (*völkisch*) has lost honor becomes politically defenseless, and then becomes enslaved also in the economic sphere.

Internationalization today means only Judaization. We in Germany have come to this: that a sixty-million people sees its destiny to lie at the will of a few dozen Jewish bankers. This was possible only because our civilization had first been Judaized. The undermining of the German conception of personality by catchwords had begun long before. Ideas such as "Democracy," "Majority," "Conscience of the World," "World Solidarity," "World Peace," "Internationality of Art," etc., disintegrate our race-consciousness, breed cowardice, and so today we are bound to say that the simple Turk is more man than we are.

No salvation is possible until the bearer of disunion, the Jew, has been rendered powerless to harm.

1. We must call to account the November criminals of 1918. It cannot be that two million Germans should have fallen in vain and that afterwards one should sit down as friends at the same table with traitors. No, we do not pardon, we demand—Vengeance!

2. The dishonoring of the nation must cease. For betrayers of their Fatherland and informers the gallows is the proper place. Our streets and squares shall once more bear the names of our heroes; they shall not be named after Jews. In the Question of Guilt we must proclaim the truth.

3. The administration of the State must be cleared of the rabble which is fattened at the stall of the parties.

4. The present laxity in the fight against usury must be abandoned. Here the fitting punishment is the same as that for the betrayers of their Fatherland.

5. We must demand a great enlightenment on the subject of the Peace Treaty. With thoughts of love? No! but in holy hatred against those who have ruined us.

6. The lies which would veil from us our misfortunes must cease. The fraud of the present money-madness must be shown up. That will stiffen the necks of us all.

7. As foundation for a new currency the property of those who are not of our blood must do service. If families who have lived in Germany for a thousand years are now expropriated, we must do the same to the Jewish usurers.

8. We demand immediate expulsion of all Jews who have entered Germany since 1914, and of all those, too, who through trickery on the Stock Exchange or through other shady transactions have gained their wealth.

9. The housing scarcity must be relieved through energetic action; houses must be granted to those who deserve them. Eisner said in 1918 that we had no right to demand the return of our prisoners—he was only saying openly what all Jews were thinking. People who so think must feel how life tastes in a concentration camp!

Extremes must be fought by extremes. Against the infection of materialism, against the Jewish pestilence we must hold aloft a flaming ideal. And if others speak of the World and Humanity we say the Fatherland—and only the Fatherland!

Hitler was imprisoned in 1923, following the failure of an uprising in Munich. While in prison he wrote *Mein Kampf,* the book which was to serve as the basic text of Nazi ideology.

It is too easy to dismiss these writings as the scribbling of a madman. The pursuit of an understanding of history compels us to see this work as a link in the chain of important documents which subsequently led to the destruction of one-third of world Jewry and embroiled mankind in a world war. The selections presented here indicate the definite formulation of Hitler's anti-Semitism which was already voiced in his early speeches. The first selection shows Hitler's concern with racial purity which he felt so necessary for the German state. Racism became a cornerstone of his future planning.

RACIAL THEORY AND PLANNING

The folkish state must make up for what everyone else today has neglected in this field. It must set race in the center of all life. It must take care to keep it pure. It must declare the child to be the most precious treasure of the people. It must see to it that only the healthy beget children; that there is only one disgrace: despite one's own sickness and deficiencies, to bring children into the world, and the highest honor to renounce doing so. And conversely it must be considered reprehensible: to withhold healthy children from the nation. Here the state must act as the guardian of a millennial future in the face of which the wishes and the selfishness of the individual must appear as nothing and submit. It must put the most modern medical means in the service of this knowledge. It must declare unfit for propagation all who are in any way visibly sick or who have inherited a disease and can therefore pass it on, and put this into actual practice. Conversely, it must take care that the fertility of the healthy woman is not limited by the financial irresponsibility of a state regime which turns the blessing of children into a curse for the parents. It must put an end to that lazy, nay criminal, indifference with which the social premises for a fecund family are treated today, and must instead feel itself to be the highest guardian of this most precious blessing of a people. Its concern belongs more to the child than to the adult.

Those who are physically and mentally unhealthy and unworthy must not perpetuate their suffering in the body of their children. In this the folkish state must perform the most gigantic educational task. And some day this will seem to be a greater deed than the most victorious wars of our present bourgeois era. By education it must teach the individual that it is no disgrace, but only a misfortune deserving of pity, to be sick and weakly, but that it is a crime and hence at the same time a disgrace to dishonor one's misfortune by one's own egotism in burdening innocent creatures with it; that by comparison it bespeaks a nobility of highest idealism and the most admirable humanity if the innocently sick, renouncing a child of his own, bestows his love and tenderness upon a poor, unknown young scion of his own nationality, who with his health promises to become some day a powerful member of a powerful community. And in this educational work the state must perform the purely intellectual complement of its practical activity. It must act in this sense without regard to understanding or lack of understanding, approval or disapproval.

A prevention of the faculty and opportunity to procreate on the part of the physically degenerate and mentally sick, over a period of only six hundred years, would not only free humanity from an immeasurable misfortune, but would lead to a recovery which today seems scarcely conceivable. If the fertility of the healthiest bearers of the nationality is thus consciously and systematically promoted, the result will be a race which at least will have eliminated the germs of our present physical and hence spiritual decay.

For once a people and a state have started on this path, attention will automatically be directed to increasing the racially most valuable nucleus of the people and its fertility, in order ultimately to let the entire nationality partake of the blessing of a highly bred racial stock.

In the folkish state, finally, the folkish philosophy of life must succeed in bringing about that nobler age in which men no longer are concerned with breeding dogs, horses, and cats, but in elevating man himself, an age in which the one knowingly and silently renounces, the other joyfully sacrifices and gives.

(From *Mein Kampf*)

Mein Kampf is not a forceful philosophical statement, but it did become the basic text for Nazi state planning. Along with his views on racism, Hitler presented his most explicit view of Jews, and an explanation of his anti-Semitism. He was quick to point out that his opinion was based on reason and not emotion, and that he arrived at his decision after due deliberation. The following excerpt is pivotal to understanding the mind of Adolf Hitler.

ADOLF HITLER'S ANTI-SEMITISM

My views with regard to anti-Semitism thus succumbed to the passage of time, and this was my greatest transformation of all.

It cost me the greatest inner soul struggles, and only after months of battle between my reason and my sentiments did my reason begin to emerge victorious. Two years later, my sentiment had followed my reason, and from then on became its most loyal guardian and sentinel.

At the time of this bitter struggle between spiritual education and cold reason, the visual instruction of the Vienna streets had performed invaluable service. There came a time when I no longer, as in the first days, wandered blindly through the mighty city; now with open eyes I saw not only the buildings but also the people.

Once, as I was strolling through the Inner City, I suddenly encountered an apparition in a black caftan and black hair locks. Is this a Jew? was my first thought.

For, to be sure, they had not looked like that in Linz. I observed the man furtively and cautiously, but the longer I stared at this foreign face, scrutinizing feature for feature, the more my first question assumed a new form: Is this a German?

As always in such cases, I now began to try to relieve my doubts by books. For a few hellers I bought the first anti-Semitic pamphlets of my life. Unfortunately, they all proceeded from the supposition that in principle the reader knew or even understood the Jewish question to a certain degree. Besides, the tone for the most part was such that doubts again arose in me, due in part to the dull and amazingly unscientific arguments favoring the thesis.

I relapsed for weeks at a time, once even for months.

The whole thing seemed to me so monstrous, the accusations so boundless, that, tormented by the feat of doing injustice, I again became anxious and uncertain.

Yet, I could no longer very well doubt that the objects of my study were not Germans of a special religion, but a people in themselves; for since I had begun to concern myself with this question and to take cognizance of the Jews, Vienna appeared to me in a different light than before. Wherever I went, I began to see Jews, and the more I saw, the more sharply they became distinguished in my eyes from the rest of humanity. Particularly the Inner City and the districts north of the Danube Canal swarmed with a people which even outwardly had lost all resemblance to Germans.

And whatever doubts I may still have nourished were finally dispelled by the attitude of a portion of the Jews themselves.

Among them there was a great movement, quite extensive in Vienna, which came out sharply in confirmation of the national character of the Jews: this was the *Zionists*.

It looked, to be sure, as though only a part of the Jews approved this viewpoint, while the great majority condemned and inwardly rejected such a formulation. But when examined more closely, this appearance dissolved itself into an unsavory vapor of pretexts advanced for mere reasons of expediency, not to say lies. For the so-called liberal Jews did not reject the Zionists as non-Jews, but only as Jews with an impractical, perhaps even dangerous, way of publicly avowing their Jewishness.

Intrinsically they remained unalterably of one piece.

In short time this apparent struggle between Zionistic and liberal Jews disgusted me; for it was false through and through, founded on lies and scarcely in keeping with the moral elevation and purity always claimed by this people.

The cleanliness of this people, moral and otherwise, I must say, is a point in itself. By their very exterior you could tell that these were no lovers of water, and, to your distress, you often knew it with your eyes closed. Later I often grew sick to my stomach from the smell of these caftan-wearers. Added to this, there was their unclean dress and their generally unheroic appearance.

All this could scarcely be called very attractive; but it became positively repulsive when, in addition to their physical uncleanliness, you discovered the moral stains on this "chosen people."

In a short time I was made more thoughtful than ever by my slowly rising insight into the type of activity carried on by the Jews in certain fields.

Was there any form of filth or profligacy, particularly in cultural life, without at least one Jew involved in it?

If you cut even cautiously into such an abscess, you found, like a maggot in a rotting body, often dazzled by the sudden light—a kike!

What had to be reckoned heavily against the Jews in my eyes was when I became acquainted with their activity in the press, art, literature, and the theater. All the unctuous reassurances helped little or nothing. It sufficed to look at a billboard, to the names of the men behind the horrible trash they advertised, to make you think hard for a long time to come. This was pestilence, spiritual pestilence, worse than the Black Death of olden times, and the people was being infected with it! It goes without saying that the lower the intellectual level of one of these art manufacturers, the more unlimited his fertility will be, and the scroundrel ends up like a garbage separator, splashing his filth in the face of humanity. And bear in mind that there is no limit to their number; bear in mind that for one Goethe Nature easily can foist on the world ten thousand of these scribblers who poison men's souls like germ-carriers of the worse sort, on their fellow men.

It was terrible, but not to be overlooked, that precisely the Jew, in tremendous numbers, seemed chosen by Nature for this shameful calling.

Is this why the Jews are called the "chosen people"?

I now begin to examine carefully the names of all the creators of unclean products in public artistic life. The result was less and less favorable for my previous attitude toward the Jews. Regardless how my sentiment might resist, my reason was forced to draw its conclusions.

The fact that nine-tenths of all literary filth, artistic trash, and theatrical idiocy can be set to the account of a people, constituting hardly one hundredth of all the country's inhabitants, could simply not be talked away; it was the plain truth.

And I now began to examine my beloved "world press" from this point of view.

And the deeper I probed, the more the object of my former admiration shriveled. The style became more and more unbearable; I could not help rejecting the content as inwardly shallow and banal; the objectivity of exposition now seemed to me more akin to lies than honest truth; and the writers were—Jews.

A thousand things which I had hardly seen before now struck my notice, and others, which had previously given me food for thought, I now learned to grasp and understand.

I now saw the liberal attitude of this press in a different light; the lofty tone in which it answered attacks and its method of killing them with silence now revealed itself to me as a trick as clever as it was treacherous; the transfigured raptures of their theatrical critics were always directed at Jewish writers, and their disapproval never struck anyone but Germans. The gentle pinpricks against William II revealed its methods by their persistency, and so did its commendation of French culture and civilization. The trashy content of the short story now appeared to me as outright indecency, and in the language I detected the accents of a foreign people; the sense of the whole thing was so obviously hostile to Germanism that this could only have been intentional.

But who had an interest in this?

Was all this a mere accident?

Gradually I became uncertain.

The development was accelerated by insights which I gained into a number of other matters. I am referring to the general view of ethics and morals which was quite openly exhibited by a large part of the Jews, and the practical application of which could be seen.

Here again the streets provided an object lesson of a sort which was sometimes positively evil.

The relation of the Jews to prostitution and, even more, to the white-slave traffic, could be studied in Vienna as perhaps in no other city of Western Europe, with the possible exception of the southern French ports. If you walked at night through the streets and alleys of Leopoldstadt, at every step, you witnessed proceedings which remained concealed from the majority of the German people until the War gave the soldiers on the eastern front occasion to see similar things, or, better expressed, forced them to see them.

When thus for the first time I recognized the Jew as the cold-hearted, shameless, and calculating director of this revolting vice traffic in the scum of the big city, a cold shudder ran down my back.

But then a flame flared up within me. I no longer avoided discussion of the Jewish question; no, now I sought it. And when I learned to look for the Jew in all branches of cultural and artistic life and its various manifestations, I suddenly encountered him in a place where I would least have expected to find him.

When I recognized the Jew as the leader of the Social Democracy, the scales dropped from my eyes. A long soul struggle had reached its conclusion.

(From *Mein Kampf*)

FIVE

Nazi Legislation

By April 1933 the German Jewish community was fully aware of the anti-Semitic Nazi program. They had read *Mein Kampf,* and had heard the campaign speeches and slogans of Adolf Hitler. Their initial reaction was to wait and see how the new Nazi government would act now that it had political power. The Jews of Germany felt themselves an integrated part of German life and society, and unlike the student of history who can look back at what happened, they had no way of anticipating the catastrophe which the future held for them. Like all citizens who are rooted in their country and its culture, the idea of separating from a familiar world was a difficult one to entertain.

Living in a modern political state had led the German Jews to believe that there is a gap between what may appear to be exaggerated campaign promises, and the actual implementation of a particular political program. The notion that power leads to responsibility had been a mainstay of political reality, and despite the discomfort of the campaign rhetoric they seemed to feel that Hitler's rise to power would give him a sense of responsibility towards all German citizens as well as a modification of his often-articulated anti-Semitism.

In *Mein Kampf* and in his speeches prior to and following his election, Hitler had said quite clearly that he saw the Jews as a separate and dangerous group. He devised three options for dealing with them: (1) destroy them, (2) expel them, or (3) isolate them. Of these options, expulsion and isolation were part of the Jewish collective memory. The Middle Ages were filled with incidents of both expulsion and isolation, but at no time had the idea of total destruction been devised and implemented as an instrument of social planning. It is clear that Hitler had not come to a definite decision in his plan for the Jews at the time of his ascent to power in 1933. The German Jews were correct in feeling that, while he had revealed his feelings, he had not decided on a course of action. By 1935, however, the development of his program can be seen in the Nuremberg Laws which led to a rigid isolation of the Jewish community. These laws became the basis of all later German regulations for depriving people of their rights because of their Jewishness. The Nuremberg Laws of September, 1935 were followed by others, such as the Defense Law of May 21, 1935, which excluded Jews from military service; the Law Concerning Officials of January 26, 1937, which prevented Jews from holding public office; and the Seventh Decree to the Reich Citizenship Law of December 5, 1938, which removed Jews from the Civil Service.

The following selection taken from the 1935 Nuremberg Laws is an undramatic statement in the legal terminology of a sovereign state. The very notion of framing such legislation as just another section of the governmental law code of a modern industrial state demands that we study it carefully.

Law for the Protection of the German Blood and the German Honor

Imbued with the conviction that the purity of the German blood is prerequisite for the future existence of the German people, and animated with the unbending will to ensure the existence of the German nation for all the future, the Reichstag has unanimously adopted the following law, which is hereby proclaimed:

No. 1. (1) Marriages between Jews and state members *(Staatsangehöriger)* of German or cognate blood are forbidden. Marriages concluded despite this law are invalid, even if they are concluded abroad in order to circumvent this law. (2) Only the State Attorney may initiate the annulment suit.

No. 2. Extramarital relations between Jews and state members of German or cognate blood are prohibited.

No. 3. Jews must not engage domestic help in their households among state members of German or cognate blood, who are under 45 years.

No. 4. (1) The display of the Reich and national flag and the showing of the national colors by Jews is prohibited. (2) However, the display of the Jewish colors is permitted to them. The exercise of this right is placed under the protection of the state.

No. 5. (1) Whosoever acts in violation of the prohibition of No. 1, will be punished with penal servitude. (2) Whosoever acts in violation of No. 2, will be punished with either imprisonment or penal servitude. (3) Whosoever acts in violation of No. 3 or No. 4, will be punished by imprisonment up to one year, with a fine, or with either of these penalties.

No. 7. This law goes into effect on the day following promulgation, except for No. 3, which shall go into force on January 1, 1936.

The Reich Citizenship Law (September 15, 1935) provided that only one who is of German or cognate blood could be a citizen. Jews remained subjects but not citizens of Germany.

7. The Reich Citizenship Law

No. 2. (1) A Reich citizen *(Reichsbürger)* is only the state member *(Staatsangehöriger)* who is of German or cognate blood, and shows through his conduct that he is both desirous and fit to serve in faith the German people and Reich. (3) The Reich citizen is the only holder of full political rights in accordance with the provisions of the laws.

8. *First Decree to the Reich Citizenship Law, November 14, 1935*

No. 4. (1) A Jew cannot be a citizen of the Reich. He cannot exercise the right to vote on political matters; he cannot hold public office. (2) Jewish officials are to be retired on December 31, 1935. In case these officials served either Germany or her allies at the front in the World War, they shall receive as a pension, until they reach their age limit, the full salary last received; they are not, however, to be promoted according to seniority. After they reach the age limit, their pension is to be calculated anew according to the salary last received, on the basis of which their pension was to be computed. (3) Affairs of religious organizations are not affected therewith. (4) The conditions of service of teachers in public Jewish schools remain unchanged until the forthcoming regulation of the Jewish school system.

No. 5. (1) A Jew is anyone who is descended from at least three full Jewish grandparents. No. 2, clause 2, sentence 2 is to be applied. (2) A Jewish state member of mixed descent (*Staatsangehöriger jüdischer Mischling*) who is descended from two full Jewish grandparents is also considered a Jew, if

(a) He belonged to the Jewish religious community at the time this law was issued or joined the community later,

(b) He was married to a Jew at the time when the law was issued, or if he married a Jew subsequently,

(c) He is the offspring of a marriage with a Jew within the meaning of clause 1, which was contracted after the Law for the Protection of German Blood and Honor of September 15, 1935, went into effect,

(d) He is the offspring of extra-marital intercourse with a Jew, within the meaning of clause 1, and will be born out of wedlock after July 31, 1936.

(From the Nuremberg Laws, issued September 15, 1935, and Berlin, November 14, 1935)

Hitler felt the need to define who was a Jew. That there was a need for definition indicates the social situation of Germany Jewry. One could no longer go to a synagogue to find all of the Jews, nor could one rely solely on the status of parents. The decline in synagogue participation and the high inter-marriage rate had made such easy criteria impossible. As the documents point out, biological criteria as well as personal identity choice were to be used. The complicated social status of the Jews in Germany required a complicated legal definition. (The apartheid laws of South Africa are the closest attempt at social definition in our time, and are one of the few examples of this type of legislation in the contemporary world scene.)

These laws denied Jews their status as German citizens. In a dramatic reversal, the Jews of Germany were reduced to the situation of Jews in France in 1789-90 (see Chapter One). These laws were Hitler's total and complete repudiation of emancipation for which Jews and enlightened Christians had worked so hard.

Another aspect of the Nuremberg Laws which should be noted is the introduction of the concept of the biological health of German society. The codification of this concept in 1935 was a major step in Hitler's evolution of his anti-Semitic policies. This new policy was restricted to Germany in 1935, the only place where Hitler had power, but it foreshadows the various aspects of what was to evolve eventually as the "Final Solution."

Though the promulgation of the Nuremberg Laws figured in the development of that "Final Solution," the fact that at the time of their publication Jews were still allowed to leave Germany indicates that the final plan for total destruction had not yet been formalized in Nazi planning. Jews could leave, but the question that had to be answered was—where to go?

SIX

Unwanted!

"Where do we go?"—became the cry of German Jews between 1935-39. The state was willing to release them, provided they would abandon all of their possessions. Hitler assumed that all property and holdings were German and, therefore, belonged to the German state. Realizing the gravity of their own situation led the Jews to an almost frantic surge of activity. But despite their willingness to leave everything behind, they could not find many places willing to accept a newly disinherited people.

The problem even came to the attention of the world community of nations. Franklin Delano Roosevelt, then President of the United States, a man of humanitarian sentiment, in his determination to take the lead, called for, and convened, a little-remembered gathering, the Evian Conference in Switzerland. Roosevelt called the Conference to discuss the "refugee problem." Of course, the "refugee problem" was the euphemism for the problem of refugee German Jews. The Conference was to find ways to open immigration throughout the world to these new refugees. It was a heartbreaking failure. The only real beneficiary of the Evian Conference was the

Nazi propaganda machine which was eager and willing to tell the public how this Conference demonstrated that the world community did not want Jews any more than Germany wanted them.

One of the journalists attending this ill-fated Conference was a man named Hans Habe, who wrote a novel, *The Mission*, depicting what had gone on there. The following selection is taken from Habe's novel and is a fictionalized conversation between Roosevelt and the United States Ambassador to the Conference. Though the Conference has not yet begun it is already a foregone conclusion that the American will be elected its chairman:

THE REFUGEES

The Ambassador reported to him on the technical preparations for the Conference. As he spoke, he looked at the President's desk, which resembled the window of a toy shop. Everyone knew that Falla, the black Scotch terrier, was the President's favorite; in the course of his six years' reign the President had received innumerable Fallas—Fallas of china and glass and bronze, of leather and wood. Among documents and folders there also stood other toys—letter openers in the shape of daggers, models of old coaches, pens with batteries, musical cigar boxes. The Ambassador was already finding it hard to resist feeling touched by this sight—the President must have been cheated of his childhood, perhaps that was why he had the power to move hearts.

"Don't underestimate the difficulties, Mr. President," said the Ambassador, after hearing that the Conference would undoubtedly elect him its chairman. "We are speaking of half a million German and Austrian Jews, but the exodus from Czechoslovakia has begun, Hungary and Rumania will follow; the involuntary migration of the peoples . . . "

"You are already reckoning with a Hitlerian Europe, Mr. Ambassador."

"The Jews are reckoning with it. So are the participants in the Conference. Human charity has an antipathy to high numbers."

"I thought cynicism was my privilege," smiled the President, and the Ambassador was struck by this strange smile. The President seemed to smile only with his protruding full lower lip, while his thin, hard upper lip remained unmoved.

"The world regards our humanitarianism with distrust," said the Ambassador, "and I fear this also has to do with numbers. We have raised our quota for the admission of German and Austrian refugees to twenty-seven thousand annually—a drop in the ocean. People will say that with goodwill we could solve the problem on our own."

"Tell that to the Senator from Mississippi or the Representative from Utah!"

Now the Ambassador smiled too. "I shall have to explain to the delegate from Guatemala why our generosity is prevented by the Senator from Mississippi." . . .

The Ambassador had opened his briefcase and was glancing at his papers. "Thirty-one states," he said, "have now finally accepted. So there will be thirty-two including ourselves. Nine European—England, France, Switzerland, Belgium, Ireland, Holland—and the three Scandinavian countries. The Soviet Union has refused the invitation."

"With what explanation?"

"The Soviet Union is not in the habit of giving explanations. Since Marxism has already explained everything they have no need of explanations."

"We didn't count on Italy. Has the Vatican replied?"

"The Holy Father will send an observer."

"That means a refusal. Without explanation, I presume. The Catholic Church has already explained everything."

"Pius XI is eighty and seriously ill. He pointed out the 'Omens of Disaster' in his encyclical of May, nineteen hundred and thirty-two." The Ambassador continued quickly. "Divided Spain is sabotaging the Conference, the Loyalists fear concessions to Franco, Franco fears concessions to the Loyalists. The Little Entente and the Balkans are standing aside—they either have anti-Semitic governments or they fear Germany. The German Reich looks upon the Conference as a hostile act. That is illogical . . ."

"Not at all," interrupted the President. "It confirms my surmise that Germany doesn't want to get rid of its Jews, but to destroy them."

> "I must speak frankly to you, Mr. President," said the Ambassador, without reacting to the comment. "In the European countries there is disastrous unemployment. France is flooded with Spanish refugees. Palestine could absorb a considerable contingent of Jews, but England has no interest in strengthening the Zionists and tilting the balance in that divided country against the Arabs. The nineteen Latin-American states are in economic difficulties, some of them have influential German minorities, many sympathize with Hitler, almost all of them feel envy and the traditional aversion toward us. Where there is no race hatred, as in Brazil, Haiti or the Dominican Republic, there are religious prejudices. There remain Canada, Australia, and New Zealand; but the refugee question will offer them a welcome opportunity of demonstrating that solidarity with Britain which is for the most part so shaky."

(From Hans Habe, *The Mission*)

As this fictionalized account indicates, the destruction of the Jews was, indeed, the Nazi goal by that date. There were possible places of refuge—Western Europe, South America, the United States, and Palestine—but, as this excerpt points out, each area, because of either political or economic self interest, was unwilling to accept the Jewish refugees. Even Roosevelt, with all of his power and prestige, was incapable of overcoming Congressional resistance to new immigration, and was unwilling to present this major moral issue for resolution. The only victor at this Conference were the Nazis. They not only used this failure as propaganda, but now felt that they could act with impunity because the world had just said quite clearly that it was not concerned about Jews.

SEVEN

Murder

Feeling certain that world opinion would not be concerned, the Nazis began a program of mass killings of Jews. At this early stage the Nazis had not yet considered using technology for assistance; they resorted to simple mass murder. The following testimony, taken from Document 2999-ps, submitted to the International Military Tribunal at the Nuremberg Trial of War Criminals, conveys this aspect of the Holocaust with vivid detail.

TESTIMONY FROM THE NUREMBERG TRIAL

I, Hermann Friedrich Graebe, declare under oath:

From September 1941 until January 1944 I was manager and engineer in charge of a branch office in Sdolbunow, Ukraine, of the Solingen building firm of Josef Jung. In this capacity it was my job to visit the building sites of the firm. Under contract to an army construction office, the firm had orders to erect grain storage buildings on the former airport of Dubno, Ukraine.

On 5 October 1942, when I visited the building office at Dubno, my foreman, Hubert Moennikes of 21 Aussenmuehlenweg, Hamburg-Haarburg, told me that in the vicinity of the site, Jews from Dubno had been shot in three large pits, each about 30 meters long and 3 meters deep. About 1500 persons had been killed daily. All of the 5000 Jews who had still been living in Dubno before the pogrom were to be liquidated. As the shootings had taken place in his presence he was still much upset.

Thereupon I drove to the site, accompanied by Moennikes and saw near it great mounds of earth, about 30 meters long and 2 meters high. Several trucks stood in front of the mounds. Armed Ukrainian militia drove the people off the trucks under the supervision of an SS man. The militia men acted as guards on the trucks and drove them to and from the pit. All these people had the regulation yellow patches on the front and back of their clothes, and thus could be recognized as Jews.

Moennikes and I went direct to the pits. Nobody bothered us. Now I heard rifle shots in quick succession, from behind one of the earth mounds. The people who had got off the trucks—men, women, and children of all ages—had to undress upon the orders of an SS man, who carried a riding or dog whip. They had to put down their clothes in fixed places, sorted according to shoes, top clothing, and underclothing. I saw a heap of shoes of about 800 to 1000 pairs, great piles of under-linen and clothing. Without screaming or weeping these people undressed, stood around in family groups, kissed each other, said farewells and waited for a sign from another SS man, who stood near the pit, also with a whip in his hand. During the 15 minutes that I stood near the pit I heard no complaint or plea for mercy. I watched a family of about 8 persons, a man and woman, both about 50 with their children of about 1, 8, and 10, and two grown-up daughters of about 20 to 24. An old woman with snow-white hair was holding the 1-year-old child in her arms and singing to it, and tickling it. The child was cooing with delight. The couple were looking on with tears in their eyes. The father was holding the hand of a boy about 10 years old and speaking to him softly; the boy was fighting his tears. The father pointed toward the sky, stroked his head, and the next moment the SS man at the pit shouted something to his comrade. The latter counted off about 20 persons and instructed them to go behind the earth mound. Among them was the family, which I have mentioned. I well remember a girl, slim and with black hair, who, as she passed close to me pointed to herself and said, "23." I walked around the mound and found myself confronted by a tremendous grave. People were closely wedged together and lying on top of each other so that only their heads were visible. Nearly all had blood running over their shoulders from their heads. Some of the people shot were still moving. Some were lifting their arms and turning their heads to show that they were still alive. The pit was already 2/3 full; I estimated that it already contained about 1000 people. I looked for the man who did the shooting. He was an SS man, who sat at the edge of the narrow end of the pit, his feet dangling into the pit. He had a tommy gun on his knees and was smoking a cigarette. The people, completely naked, went down some steps which were cut in the clay wall of the pit and clambered over the heads of the people lying there, to the place to which the SS man directed them. They lay down in front of the dead or injured people; some caressed those who were still alive and spoke to them in a low voice. Then I heard a series of shots. I looked into the pit and saw that the bodies were twitching or the heads lying already motionless on top of the bodies that lay before them. Blood was running from their necks. I was surprised that I was not ordered away, but I saw that there were two or three postmen in uniform nearby. The next batch was approaching already. They went down into the pit, lined themselves up against the previous victims and were shot. When I walked back, around the mound I noticed another truck-load of people which had just arrived. This time it included sick and infirm persons. An old, very thin woman with terribly thin legs was undressed by others who were already naked, while two people held her up. The woman appeared to be paralyzed. The naked people carried the woman around the mound. I left with Moennikes and drove in my car back to Dubno.

On the morning of the next day, when I again visited the site, I saw about 30 naked people lying near the pit—about 30 to 50 meters away from it. Some of them were still alive; they looked straight in front of them with a fixed stare and seemed to notice neither the chilliness of the morning nor the workers of my firm who stood around. A girl of about 20 spoke to me and asked me to give her clothes, and help her escape. At that moment we heard a fast car approach and noticed that it was an SS detail. I moved away to my site. 10 minutes later we heard shots from the vicinity of the pit. The Jews still alive had been ordered to throw the corpses into the pit—then they had themselves to lie down in this to be shot.

The decision to destroy the Jewish people had been taken.

EIGHT

Isolation

In his writings and speeches, Hitler had proposed several "solutions" to the Jewish problem; one had been the isolation of the Jews from the society. Soon, the brutal, but as yet, primitive destruction of the Jews was underway. Now in addition to the killings in Germany, the isolation of Polish Jews was undertaken as early as the fall of 1939. Jews were moved into large cities, placed in sealed-off, isolated areas where the basic requirements for life were meager and inadequate. The creation of these ghettos introduced a tragic epoch in Jewish history. The ghettos were filled with heroism, self-sacrifice, and self-respect in spite of the horrible reality of life. Several diaries of ghetto life with its day by day struggle for self respect have been preserved. The best known of these was written by Emmanuel Ringelblum, a Jew who had received a Ph.D. in history from the University of Warsaw. Ringelblum, who became a leader in the Warsaw ghetto, was murdered by the Nazis in Warsaw in 1944.

EMMANUEL RINGELBLUM

Today, Saturday the 12th of October, was dreadful. The loudspeaker announced the division of the city into three parts: a German quarter, encompassing midtown and Nowy Swiat Street; a Polish quarter; and a Jewish quarter. By the end of October, everyone but the Germans has to move over into the quarter assigned them, without taking their furniture. Black melancholy reigned in our courtyard. The mistress of the house had been living there some thirty-seven years, and now has to leave her furniture behind. Thousands of Christians' businesses are going to be ruined—heard about a police chief who jumped out of a streetcar at the sight of students from Konarski's school attacking Jews, ran after them, and fired in the air. Don't know how it ended.

There are 140,000 Poles living in the quarter assigned to Jews; 60,000 Jews outside that quarter. Heard from some Poles of a sentence executed on Poles in Torun: The prisoners were bound to a motorcycle, their hands and feet were tied (and the motorcycle was driven) until they breathed their last. Gradually, a Ghetto is being established. All telegrams have to be dispatched through the Jewish Council; they handle train tickets, too. The Jews have received a bitter "gift" this Yom Kippur. Some people maintain that it is even worse for the Poles, who have a great many business undertakings in the Ghetto. On Walowa Street the Jewish merchants have solved the security problem by a very simple method: There's a German in uniform sitting in a cafe. He gets 100 zlotys a day; his duty is to come to the aid of any merchant on the street threatened with robbery. The fact that Jews of Praga may not go out of the Ghetto after seven o'clock at night is a great (economic) blow to the Jewish populace.

Today, Sunday, the 13th of October, left a peculiar impression. It's become clear that 140,000 Jews from the south of Warsaw and the Praga suburb will have to leave their homes and move into the Ghetto. All the suburbs have been emptied of Jews, and 140,000 Christians will have to leave the Ghetto quarter. The question of what's to happen to the Christian businesses has not yet been clarified. All day people were moving furniture. The Jewish Council was besieged by hundreds of people wanting to know what streets were included in the Ghetto. A group of assimilated teachers are said to have gone to the Polish (school) inspectors for support against the Jews who wished to introduce the teaching of Yiddish in the folk schools.

ISOLATION 45

The porters take advantage of every opportunity to make money. When the house at 31 Dzielna Street was closed down, they threw the things in the house over a fence. The porters locked the gates and demanded 2-3 zlotys per package retrieved. The removal of the Jews from the suburbs as well as from poverty-stricken Praga signifies their complete ruination; they will not even have the money to resettle. Some people are having terrible trouble with their Christian servants... They can't be laid off without the permission of the labor exchange, so they do whatever they want. There have been cases of servants putting on their mistresses' things. The Christians who live on the banks of the Vistula and work the sand banks say they won't move, though threatened with bloodshed. Today was a terrifying day; the sight of Jews moving their old rags and bedding made a horrible impression. Though forbidden to remove their furniture, some Jews did it. There were cases of vehicles containing furniture being stopped and taken away. This is what happened in Wartegoj last year. A congregation of Jews were ordered to bury the president of the Jewish Council, or maybe it was the rabbi of the town. They had reached his throat before the Others explained that it was only a joke. The Jew shook the dirt off and said: "The earth take them!" Heard that the Others have threatened that if typhus should spread the Ghetto will be closed. The Jewish Council announced the recruitment of 1,000 Jewish policemen, honorary at first. The complete impotence of the Council. Two weeks back, the city fathers congratulated Adam Czerniakow on his victory: He had staved off a Ghetto. As late as Friday, i.e., a day before the decree, the Council announced that no Ghetto was in prospect. Some Christian landlords in Praga will not permit anything to be removed from the apartments until rent is paid for October. Others will allow nothing to be removed. "Happy Corner." That's what the Jews call the newspaper page that tells about "marmalade"— the German casualty lists. S.S. men were removing furniture from a house on Ciepla Street. Across the way, a Jewish troupe was singing and playing music. The S.S. men ordered the troup to play a waltz and dance in the middle of the street. The well-dressed Jews who came along were ordered to give 5 zlotys for the entertainment; poorly dressed Jews, 10 groschen and more. They seized several women, took them into a cellar. There they forced them to pluck feathers. After the women had finished, they stripped them naked and gave each of them thirty blows. According to the new law promulgated by Dr. Fischer, governor of the Warsaw district, Poles may remain living in the German quarter of the city, but they may not move into it. It is feared that the Poles will refuse to move out of the new Jewish quarter. Moving out of the Polish quarter is attended with great difficulty. Some Christians say they will not move out. They'd rather burn their houses down. Jews were driven out of Czestochowa into a neighborhood near the graveyard, where only a very few of them can live. In Otwock the introduction of a Ghetto has been deferred temporarily.

Today the rumor spread that there would be no sick fund. There is talk of a public-morals police force in Warsaw. The city is placarded with white cards advertising apartments for exchange between Jews and Christians. The whole wall near the apartment office of the Jewish Council is white. The Poles are up to all kinds of tricks to increase the number of houses in the Polish quarter. For example, they wall up the gates of houses facing on Jewish neighborhoods; the gates facing Polish neighborhoods of the very same houses are left open. The rumor is rife among Polish *hoi polloi* that the Jews have collected 5 million zlotys and given it to the Others so as to be given the larger plazas, wider streets, and so forth. The Jews in the German section of Warsaw are particularly unfortunate, because they have no chance of exchanging apartments. Some Poles pick the Jewish apartments they want and appear with requisition orders from the magistracy. This tactic deprives Jews of the right to exchange apartments with Christians. A Ghetto was instituted in Pruszkow. Some Jews don't open up when the Others come. One man was praying, and in the middle of the Eighteen Benedictions, which he didn't want to interrupt. So, unable to wait any longer, They left. About Brenner*: What did Hitler and Mussolini talk about? "Benito zebito, O Adolfo, we need helpo, O sweet Duce, we are kaputshee. Heil Hitler I am looking for a middlemanner. If so, Mussolini, you are a swiney. If you have to complaino, go to Ciano, It was R . . . b . . . p (Ribbentrop) who did this to me, the goddamn s.o.b."

*The meeting between Hitler and Mussolini at Brenner Pass.

October 20

... how the Jewish police have taken over the police service. They direct traffic in the street. They've put things straight on Karmelicka Street. They're already sitting around in the commissariats, though the Polish police are still in charge. On the 31st the Poles are due to leave. It's reported that a large transport of sugar was moved through Chlodna Street. Each of the guards got five thousand. Though Germans have to have passes to enter the Ghetto, a number of streets were robbed today again and bedding and the like taken away. Long lines standing in front of the drug stores, which are being simply sold out. The courtyards too are buying large amounts... The dearth of medications in the Lodz Ghetto, where a spoonful of castor oil was worth a fortune during the dysentery attack.

The people who have come here from Lodz, experienced in Ghetto life, have concentrated on buying up large quantities of produce. They also buy big amounts of wood, rather than coal.

Today there was a vicious article in the Polish rag (New Warsaw Courier) about the Sabbath Gentiles who serve as the Jews' catspaws, bringing produce into the Ghetto. A series of such articles is being published—with photographs of the persons involved.

Heard that the group that was impressed to work in Polaw under Jewish supervision have found good conditions there. They earn 3 zlotys 20, of which 1 and 20 goes toward maintenance. The rest is for the family. They live in stone barracks; the place is kept warm; on arrival they received breakfast. The Jews from Henrikow and neighboring towns were sent into the countryside; the same in the area around Radomsk. People prefer to work in Okencia. On the way back from work, they buy a couple of breads and make some money selling the bread in the Ghetto. The *righteous Gentile* cursed out the Polish police chief of Grochow for putting the *chalutzim* in prison; made him personally responsible if a hair of their heads was touched. Bought a Dutch cow for them. Has great feeling for Jews who work on the land.

The Jewish Council is maneuvering so as not to have to create a food-supply office itself for the Ghetto, but to have the city magistracy continue to handle this function. The Poles are in accord with this; one of their head officials in the magistracy has promised to help in this matter. Janusz Korczak arrested for not wearing an arm band. Today the Germans declared that no potatoes would be allowed to enter the Ghetto, because the Jews have large hoards of them. We are to receive potatoes later.

Today, the 23rd of October, another announcement over the loud-speaker that Walicow and Zeglana Streets have been excluded from the Ghetto. At the same time, news that the deadline for moving into the Ghetto has been postponed until after the 31st of October, i.e., until the 15th of November. People are walking around crazy with anxiety because they don't know where to move to. Not a single street is sure of being assigned to the Ghetto, but every street has something that puts it in jeopardy. On Zeglana Street it was Ulrich's factory that decided for its exclusion from the Ghetto. The head of the resettlement office is said to be the same Sh. (Shea Braude) infamous for having organized the Lodz Ghetto. People are fearful lest the Lodz experience be repeated in Warsaw. Today the orphanage at 6 Wolska Street sent its children, thinly dressed and barefoot, to the Society for Self-Aid offices at 5 Tlomackie Place. This was intended as a demonstration against the Jewish Council, but the children were driven away, so they overturned a few wagons. A fearful uncertainty has seized everyone. No one knows what the next day will offer. A few days ago hoodlums broke into 93 Zelazna Street and forcibly occupied some Jewish apartments. They hung up a cross and said, "Dare to touch this!"

(From Emmanuel Ringelblum, *Notes From the Warsaw Ghetto*)

Mary Berg, daughter of an American woman, lived in the Warsaw Ghetto. She survived the war, and later published her diary. This selection overlaps in time with the one by Ringelblum.

MARY BERG

December 24, 1940

Our second war—Christmas. From my window which gives on the "Aryan" side I can see Christmas trees lit up.

But little pine trees were also sold in the ghetto this morning at exorbitant prices. They were smuggled in yesterday. I saw shivering people hurrying home with the little trees pressed to their chests. These were converts or first-generation Christians whom the Nazis regard as Jews and whom they have confined in the ghetto.

December 25, 1940

Today a new group of uniformed Jewish officials appeared in the ghetto. They belong to the special Commission for the Fight Against Speculators, whose task it is to regulate the prices of various articles. For some time this organization has functioned in secret, but now it is out in the open. These officials wear the same kind of cap as the Jewish policemen, but with a green band and instead of the policemen's yellow arm bands, they wear lavender arm bands with the inscription, "Fight Against Speculators."

While the attitude of the Jewish population toward the Jewish policemen is cordial, these new officials are treated with marked reserve because they are suspected of being tools of the Gestapo. Their organization has been nicknamed "The Thirteen," because its office is at 13 Leszno Street. Its chief is Commissar Szternfeld; his main collaborators are Gancwajch, Roland Szpunt and the lawyer Szajer of Lodz.

There is another group of uniformed Jewish officials in the ghetto—the workers of the ambulance unit, who wear a blue band on their caps, and blue arm bands. Still another is the black-clad corps of undertakers employed by private companies, among which the most popular are Pinkert's next to the community building on the Grzybowska and Wittenberg's, directly across the street. Even to pass into the next world is not very easy these days. Funerals are frightfully expensive, and a lot in the overcrowded Jewish cemetery is as precious as gold.

Meanwhile life is being organized in the ghetto. Work helps one to forget everything, and it is not hard to get work here. A great number of workshops and factories have opened; they make all sorts of articles that have never before been manufactured in Warsaw.

Our theoretical group has received several invitations to give performances in cafes. We also have our own hall and intend to give regular shows two or three times a week in the afternoon. We have rented Weisman's dancing school on Panska Street, although it had an unsavory reputation before the war because the Warsaw underworld used to meet there. The inhabitants of the quarter once called this hall the "old joint." But now we have our own public, which will disregard the bad reputation of the hall and attend our shows regardless of where they are given. Moreover there is no better hall in the whole so-called Little Ghetto that lies between Sienna and Leszno Streets.

The way from the Little Ghetto to the Big Ghetto begins at the corner of Chlodna and Zelazna Streets. Only the roadway, separated from the rest of Chlodna Street by walls on each side, is considered part of the ghetto. In the middle of the street there is an exit to Zelazna Street. This exit is especially well guarded by a Nazi gendarme armed with a machine gun, and two policemen, one Jewish and one Polish.

January 2, 1941

Our New Year's shows unexpectedly drew an enormous audience. The hall was packed to capacity. Because December 31 happened to coincide with the last day of Hanukah, we have improvised a scene depicting the heroic fight of the Maccabees, which contained many timely hints. We lit eight candles on the stage. The audience applauded enthusiastically, and there was hardly a dry eye in the house.

All our matinees are a great success. Half of the receipts go to the refugee committee, for there is still an enormous flood of homeless refugees.

January 4, 1941

The ghetto is covered with deep snow. The cold is terrible and none of the apartments are heated. Wherever I go I find people wrapped up in blankets or huddling under feather beds, that is, if the Germans have not yet taken all these warm things for their own soldiers. The bitter cold makes the Nazi beasts who stand guard near the ghetto entrances even more savage than usual. Just to warm up as they lurch back and forth in the deep snow, they open fire every so often and there are many victims among the passers-by. Other guards who are bored with their duty at the gates arrange entertainment for themselves. For instance, they choose a victim from among the people who chance to go by, order him to throw himself in the snow with his face down, and if he is a Jew who wears a beard, they tear it off together with the skin until the snow is red with blood. When such a Nazi is in a bad mood, his victim may be a Jewish policeman who stands guard with him.

Yesterday I myself saw a Nazi gendarme "exercise" a Jewish policeman near the passage from the Little to the Big Ghetto on Chlodna Street. The young man finally lost his breath, but the Nazi still forced him to fall and rise until he collapsed in a pool of blood. Then someone called for an ambulance, and the Jewish policeman was put on a stretcher and carried away on a hand truck. There are only three ambulance cars for the whole ghetto, and for that reason hand trucks are mostly used. We call them rikshas.

January 10, 1941

Last night we went through several hours of mortal terror. At about 11:00 p.m. a group of Nazi gendarmes broke into the room where our house committee was holding a meeting. The Nazis searched the men, took away whatever money they found, and then ordered the women to strip, hoping to find concealed diamonds. Our subtenant, Mrs. R., who happened to be there, courageously protested, declaring that she would not undress in the presence of men. For this she received a resounding slap on the face and was searched even more harshly than the other women. The women were kept naked for more than two hours while the Nazis put their revolvers to their breasts and private parts and threatened to shoot them all if they did not disgorge dollars or diamonds. The beasts did not leave until 2:00 a.m., carrying a scanty loot of a few watches, some paltry rings, and a small sum of Polish zlotys. They did not find either diamonds or dollars. The inhabitants of the ghetto expect such attacks every night, but this does not stop the meetings of the house committees.

January 30, 1941

Today we held the inaugural meeting of the Youth Club of our block on Sienna Street. Similar clubs have been formed in all the streets of the ghetto. We have elected as president Manfred Rubin, an intelligent young German Jewish refugee, who came to Poland shortly after the war.

Engineer Stickgold greeted us in the name of the house committees of Sienna Street. He urged us to study as hard as possible and to share among ourselves not only our bread but also our knowledge. Every member of our group at once began to prepare a subject for a talk.

February 5, 1941

There is panic among the inhabitants of Sienna Street, for the rumor has spread that the street will be cut off from the ghetto, allegedly because of the extensive smuggling that is carried on here. But this is certainly not the real reason, for the same is true of all the border streets, and if one street is cut off, the smuggling will simply be transferred to the next one. The Germans themselves are circulating rumors that Sienna Street will be left to the Jewish inhabitants if they pay a contribution. This must be the real reason for the threat—the Germans want to get a large sum of money out of the inhabitants of the ghetto.

Meanwhile snow is falling slowly, and the frost draws marvelous flower patterns on the windowpanes. I dream of a sled gliding over the ice, of freedom. Shall I ever be free again? I have become really selfish. For the time being I am still warm and have food, but all around me there is so much misery and starvation that I am beginning to be very unhappy.

Sometimes I quickly snatch my coat and go out into the street. I gaze at the faces of the passers-by, blue with cold. I try to learn by heart the look of the homeless women wrapped in rags and of the children with chapped and frozen cheeks. They huddle together, hoping to find some warmth in each other. The street vendors stand in the gateways, offering candy and tobacco for sale. They carry small boxes slung over their shoulders. These boxes contain a few packages of cigarettes, and a handful of candy made without a grain of sugar and sweetened with saccharine.

Through a show window in a store I can see the reflections of various people. The spectacle is now familiar to me: a poor man enters to buy a quarter of a pound of bread and walks out. In the street he impatiently wrenches a piece off the gluey mass and puts it in his mouth. An expression of contentment spreads over his entire face, and in a moment the whole lump of bread has disappeared. Now his face expresses disappointment. He rummages in his pocket and draws out his last copper coins ... not enough to buy anything. All he can do now is to lie down in the snow and wait for death. Or perhaps go to the community administration? It is no use. Hundreds like him are already there. The woman behind the desk who receives them and listens to their story is pathetic; she smiles politely, and tells them to come back in a week. Hunger will destroy them and one morning another body of an old man with a blue face and clenched fists will be found lying in the snow.

What are the last thoughts of such people, what makes them clench their fists so tautly? Surely their last glance was cast at the window of the store across the street where they have laid themselves down to die. In that store window they see white bread, cheese, and even cakes, and they fall into their last sleep dreaming of biting into a loaf of bread.

Every day there are more such "dreamers of bread" in the streets of the ghetto. Their eyes are veiled with a mist that belongs to another world ... Usually they sit across from the windows of food stores, but their eyes no longer see the loaves that lie behind the glass, as though in some remote inaccessible heaven.

After I have taken a good look at all this, and my heart is full to the brim with grief, I return to my warm room where I can smell the appetizing odors of good food cooking. My dreams of freedom fade. I am hungry. Now my only wish is to fill my stomach.

February 15, 1941

One after another the ghetto streets have been shut off. Now only Poles are used for this work. The Nazis no longer trust the Jewish masons, who deliberately leave loose bricks in many places in order to smuggle food or to escape to the "other side" through the holes at night.

Now the walls are growing taller and taller and there are no loose bricks. The top is covered with a thick layer of clay strewn with glass splinters, intended to cut the hands of people who try to escape.

But the Jews still find ways. The sewer pipes have not been cut off, and through the openings they get in small bags of flour, sugar, cereal, and other articles. During dark nights they also take advantage of holes made in the gates to bring in food-stuffs. The removal of one brick is sufficient. Special packages are prepared to fit these holes.

There are other ways, too. Many bombed houses are situated on the border between the ghetto and the "other side." The cellars of these houses often form long tunnels that extend for three, four, or five houses. The greatest part of the smuggling is carried on through these tunnels. The Germans know this, but are unable to control the traffic.

Meanwhile the Nazis are cutting out of the ghetto the larger and more modern apartment houses. A number of streets have been split in two: one side belongs to the ghetto, the other to the "Aryan" side. In the middle of the street there is barbed wire or a wall. We tremble lest the same thing be done with Sienna Street, where we live, because the most beautiful homes in the whole quarter are on that street.

February 17, 1941

The Jewish community administration is completing its preparations for a course in machine drawing, architecture, and graphic arts. I have registered for it. I received a typewritten prospectus which explains that the course is being opened by the special permission of the German authorities and is part of the general program for training locksmiths, electrotechnicians, and other artisans from among the young Jewish people who have no trade. We all realize that the Germans' real intention is to train workers for their war industries, workers who will work without wages.

The metallurgical and related courses will be given in the community building at 26 Grzybowska Street; the courses in industrial drawing will be given at 16 Sienna Street, not far from my home. I shall not be exposed to

ISOLATION

the danger of walking many streets to get to school. The course will last six months, and the tuition fee is twenty-five zlotys a month. There are also a number of scholarships for poor but gifted pupils.

When I went to register, I saw many familiar faces, among them Mark Unger, my accompanist, and Manfred Rubin, the president of the Youth Committee of our block. There are almost six hundred candidates, although the number of vacancies is only a few dozen. Unfortunately "pull" plays a large part in the selection of students. At first I rebelled against this, but when I realized that my chances of being admitted were slight, I finally decided to resort to the same means.

(From Mary Berg, *Warsaw Ghetto: A Diary*)

NINE

The Roundup

The process of the destruction of the Jewish people had begun with mass killings and then isolation. The last phase of this plan, which came to be known as "the Final Solution," the application of technological skills to this scheme, did not become an established program until 1942. Then came something new in the whole of world history—genocide, the planned execution of an entire people.

The first phase of the well-organized and highly technological process of genocide was the systematic roundup of Jews. The following selection, taken from Alexander Donat's *The Holocaust Kingdom*, vividly depicts how this part of the program was administered.

> The roundup procedure began with cordoning off an apartment house. Ghetto police blocked all exits, and then fifteen or twenty of them, with an officer in charge, ordered all occupants into the courtyard. Here papers were checked; those who failed to pass muster were immediately loaded into a wagon. While this was going on, other policemen went through every apartment to make certain no one was hiding. At first, persons hiding

had been able to escape when discovered by paying a small bribe, but the police were growing more brutal and callous.

Eventually whole streets were sealed off at one time and everyone on the street had to have his papers checked. In the early stages of the deportations every valid *Ausweis* was scrupulously respected; this was another German ruse to give Jews false confidence in documents, an illusion which led thousands to their deaths.

In our apartment house, roundups were under the command of my former lawyer, Henryk Lande, now a captain in the Ghetto police. On one roundup when I was stopped and produced my documents for him, Lande looked it over and said softly, "If I were you, I wouldn't feel so sure that this is enough. I'd get something better." I then learned that almost from the beginning there had been a special *Ausweis*, stamped *Einsatz Reinhard*, which bore the Nazi eagle and a swastika with the inscription, "Not subject to resettlement." At that stage such an *Ausweis* was a guarantee of security.

I saw a young mother run downstairs into the street to get milk for her baby. Her husband, who worked at the *Ostbahn*, had as usual left earlier that morning. She had not bothered to dress, but was in bathrobe and slippers. An empty milk bottle in hand, she was headed for a shop where, she knew, they sold milk under the counter. She walked into Operation Reinhard. The executioners demanded her *Ausweis*. "Upstairs ... *Ostbahn* ... work certificate, I'll bring it right away."

"We've heard that one before. Have you got an *Ausweis* with you, or haven't you?"

She was dragged protesting to the wagon, scarcely able to realize what was happening. "But my baby is all alone. Milk ... " she protested. "My *Ausweis* is upstairs." Then, for the first time, she really looked at the men who were holding her and she saw where she was being dragged: to the gaping entrance at the back of a high boarded wagon with victims already jammed into it. With all her young mother's strength she wrenched herself free, and then two, and four policemen fell on her, hitting her, smashing her to the ground, picking her up again, and tossing her into the wagon like a sack. I can still hear her screaming in a half-crazed voice somewhere between a sob of utter human despair and the howl of an animal.

Another young woman I knew after much trouble finally persuaded a friend of her husband's, a man who managed a shop, to register her with his firm so that she would have an *Ausweis*. "I'm doing it for you because you're Leon's wife," the man told her, but it cost her every penny of what remained of the possessions she and her husband had owned when he had left in September, 1939. "You know I'm not taking this for myself. You understand, don't you? It's because of the others ... " Then he explained to her how the very next day she must move to the shop area, and bring her eight-year-old boy with her. There she would be safe. She needn't worry about having no money or about leaving her apartment; she must bring only the absolute necessities with her, no more than the apartment house janitor's wheelbarrow could carry in one trip; but everything would be all right.

And, indeed, she was reassured. Calmly she went about doing what she had to do, fighting for the life of her child. Her husband, she knew, would be proud of how well she had managed. Holding her little boy's hand, she told him, "Now, you mustn't be afraid. Mother is looking out for you." As she was turning the corner into the street where they lived, the little boy ran ahead as children do. He skipped around the corner before she got to it. Why had she let him do it? How could she have let her sense of danger relax even for an instant? The street seemed so calm. When she heard him scream, "Mama! Mama!" she sped around the corner and had just time enough to see a little body with a familiar striped sweater disappearing among the mass of other bodies in the wagon surrounded by police. She thanked God that she was in time to explain, that she had an *Ausweis*.

"But Madam," the police said, "how can we be sure that this is your child?"

She had not, it seems, quite understood. No more than any of us did at first. And when she finally did understand, she was beaten brutally "for resisting the authorities," but not a sound, not a sob, escaped her. The policemen showed that they were not, after all, completely heartless. By surrendering her *Ausweis* to them—a commodity more valuable than gold at that point—she was permitted to get into the wagon, too, to accompany her son to the *Umschlagplatz* and what lay beyond.

As the wagon began to move away, anyone within earshot could hear the voice of an old woman coming from beyond the boards of the van, repeating monotonously, "Tell Zalme Katz his mother was taken away ... Tell Zalme Katz his mother was taken away ... Tell Zalme Katz ... " And those who listened very carefully could also hear among the other sounds coming from the van the voice of an eight-year-old boy in a striped sweater crying, "O Daddy, why did you go away and leave us?"

All the wagons went to the *Umschlagplatz* near Stawki Street. Those selected for resettlement waited in the hospital in indescribable crowding and confusion. After a sufficient number of victims had been rounded up, usually by four or five in the afternoon, the hospital was emptied and the cattle cars filled. Gun butts and clubs drove the people into the square where two SS officers made the "final selection." The overwhelming majority, some with bundles over their shoulders and leading children by the hand, passed through the gate into the railhead proper and were then jammed into the railroad cars (capacity: 40 men or 8 horses) more than 100 people to a car; then the doors were shut and bolted from the outside.

Most able-bodied males were "rejected" by the SS officers and sent to the *Dulag* (transit camp) in Leszno Street where, if shop managers or supervisors intervened on their behalf, they were released. The very old and crippled were "rejected" too, but in another way; they were part of the German category of *Transportunfähig,* "unfit for transport," and were taken to the cemetery and shot. The entire procedure was run in a manner intended to reinforce the impression that the Resettlement Operation was genuine.

Because loading didn't usually begin before late afternoon, efforts were made to obtain the release of persons who had been rounded up during the day. Intervention by shop managers or the *Judenrat* officially, or unofficially by bribing Jewish policemen, were the methods and a well-organized network of corruption quickly grew up involving the Jewish police, Ukrainian and German guards. It was an enormously profitable business and one of the low points of Ghetto depravity, yet some individuals rounded up and taken to the *Umschlagplatz* were thus able to obtain their release as many as three or four times.

Many individuals carrying large amounts of money made no effort to buy their release when caught in the round-ups. They firmly believed in the resettlement myth and felt they would need the money where they were going. I knew one man who had a contact with the police. Although penniless himself, he arranged to be released with his brother-in-law who had also been picked up and who was rich enough to pay for both of them. But the brother-in-law refused. "At a time like this," he said, "you don't spend your money on other people. I might need this money soon to save my own life." Later, I learned from a few men who managed to escape from the cattle cars, all of which went directly to Treblinka, that just before making their escape they were refused small sums of money by men who neither wished to escape themselves nor would aid those without money who did.

(From Alexander Donat, *The Holocaust Kingdom: A Memoir*)

TEN

Systematic Destruction

The technological destruction of the Jewish people was the culmination of Hitler's program which began with the denial of their humanity, and ended with their murder. The demonic misuse of science and technology is spelled out in brutal detail in this selection, which is from the opening speech by Gideon Hausner, the prosecuting attorney at the Eichmann trial.

TECHNOLOGICAL DESTRUCTION

At Belzec, on the road between Lublin and Lvov the extermination camp was set up in the winter of 1941.

I would like to quote a description of a transport from Lvov, consisting of 6,700 people. The S.S. men and the Ukrainian assistants are already waiting at the station.

"The doors of the wagons are opened and, to the lashing of whips, the people are ordered to get out. The instructions are relayed over loudspeakers; everyone is ordered to hand over clothes and belongings—crutches and spectacles as well ... All valuables and money are handed over at the window marked 'Valuables.'

" ... The women and girls then go to a barber who, with two cuts of his scissors, shears off their hair, which is put in potato sacks ... After this the march begins. To the right and left are barbed wire fences, and at the rear scores of Ukrainians with rifles . . .

"Men, women, girls, children, babies, one-legged people, all of them naked as the day they were born, march together. At the corner, before the entrance to the building, stands a smiling S.S. man who declares in an ingratiating voice: 'No harm will befall you.'

" 'All you have to do,' he says, 'is to breathe in deeply. This strengthens the lungs; inhalation is necessary as a means of disinfection.' He is asked what will happen to the women and answers that the men will, of course, have to work at road and housing construction. The women, he says, will not have to work. They may, if they want, help in the kitchen or do housework . . . For a number of men there still lingers a flicker of hope, sufficient to make them march without resistance to the death chambers. The majority know with certainty what is to be their fate. The horrible, all pervading stench reveals the truth. Then they climb some small steps and behold the reality. Silent mothers hold their babies to their breasts, naked; there are many children of all ages, naked. They hesitate but nevertheless proceed towards the death chambers, most of them without a word, pushed by those behind, chased by the whips of S.S. men. A woman of about 40 curses the chief of the murderers, crying that the blood of her children will be on his head. Wirth, an S.S. officer, himself strikes her across the face with five lashes of the whip, and she disappears into the gas chamber. Many pray . . . The S.S. officers squeeze people into the chambers. 'Fill them up well,' orders Wirth. The naked people stand on each other's feet. About seven to eight hundred people are in an area of about a hundred square yards. The doors close. The rest of the transport stands waiting, naked . . . In the winter too, they stand waiting naked . . . But the diesel engine is not functioning . . . 50 minutes pass by, 70 minutes. The people in the death chambers remain standing. Their weeping is heard. S.S. Sturmbannfuehrer Professor Dr. Pfannenstiel, lecturer on hygiene at Marburg University, remarks: 'Just like a synagogue . . . ' Only after two hours and 49 minutes does the diesel engine begin to work. Many have already died, as can be seen through the small window. Twenty-eight minutes later a few are still alive. After thirty-two minutes all are dead ... Jewish workers open the doors on the other side ... The dead, having nowhere to fall, stand like pillars of basalt. Even in death families may be seen standing pressed together, clutching hands. It is only with difficulty that the bodies are separated in order to clear the place for the next load. The blue corpses covered with sweat and urine ... babies and bodies of children, are thrown out. But there is no time! A couple of workers are busy with the mouths of the dead, opening them with iron pegs. 'With gold to the left, without gold to the right,' is the order. Others search in the private parts of the bodies for gold and diamonds ... Wirth points to a full preserves tin and exclaims, 'Lift it up, and see how much gold there is ... '"

The killings in Auschwitz were carried out by every method: shooting, hanging and beating, but mainly in the massive gas chambers. Here once again, we are confronted with the signboards: "Washing and Disinfection Rooms." In each such chamber 2,000 people were herded together for a "shower." The "shower" was a flow of poison gas which the S.S. men introduced with their own hands. The death factory operated unceasingly. The extermination of 2,000 people lasted 25 minutes, after which the bodies were taken to one of the four huge furnaces. When there was no room in the furnaces the bodies were burned in the open.

Here too the hair was shorn, the teeth extracted, and the rings removed. About 40 people were employed to handle the teeth alone, and day by day pounds of gold were melted down, sometimes as much as 26 pounds a day. At first, the victims' ashes were buried in pits, but later they were thrown into the Vistula.

At Auschwitz, medical experiments were made on human beings as if they were guinea pigs. Parts of female organs were cut out, or limbs were subjected to X-rays until the unfortunate creatures writhed in pain prior to their death. Men were castrated; experiments were made on the effects of paraffin and petrol injections on human skin, and the effects of chemical substances on mental resistance. Associated with Auschwitz is a collection of skeletons found at Strassburg by Allied soldiers when they entered that city in 1944. We shall prove that, at

Eichmann's orders, 150 Auschwitz prisoners were "supplied" for death in the Natzweiler camp in Germany, so that their skeletons might be sent for anthropological research to the S.S. Institute of Race Research, which had requested skulls of "Jewish Communist Commissars."

The prisoners who were brought to the camp and those who were not destined for immediate extermination would go through a quarantine process. Here the first selection of prisoners was made—by starvation and torture. Sometimes people were held in quarantine for days and weeks. Thousands of people were kept in stables; frequently there was not enough room in the stables and people were left in the open—in winter in the snow and mud. At parades the prisoners would be ordered to stand from evenings until noon the following day without moving. They had to sing at the command of the "kapos" and to carry out frightful "physical exercises," crawling, standing and rolling.

In the work-camp, the working day would begin at 4:30 a.m. The slaves would go out to work to the sound of the camp band and return in the evening, exhausted, wounded and carrying their fellows who had been killed by the guards.

The methods of punishment at Auschwitz would not have shamed the cruelest barbarians in history. Beating on the naked body was a comparatively light punishment. Water was poured into people's ears, fingernails were pulled out, and prisoners starved until they went out of their minds. In the bunker of those sentenced for punishment by starvation a dead prisoner was found, and bent over—a second prisoner, also dead, holding the liver from the corpse of the first. He had died while tearing at the liver of a fellow human being. The Nazi contribution to twentieth century European culture was the reintroduction of cannibalism.

Hunger reigned supreme in Auschwitz. The prisoners received only a third of the minimum human requirements of food; even after their liberation hundreds of survivors died from exhaustion and undernourishment.

The Germans tried to cover up their tracks and even to erase the memory of the hell they had created. The burnings of the bodies in the crematoria began in 1942 under an order transmitted by Eichmann through Standardtenfuehrer Blobel. Afterwards, as a prelude to the dismantling of the camp, they changed the names of the places, turned crematoria into air-raid shelters, demolished furnaces, transformed execution sheds into sham clinics, burned documents and books. In the confusion of the demolitions, in early 1945, a hut was burned down together with all the sick prisoners in it. Some of the installations were blown up. Other prisoners were evacuated in a dreadful route march to the West.

The Nazis believed that their crimes would not be revealed, that their secret would remain intact. But the secret of these atrocities has been laid bare, and we must fulfill the dying injunction of an anonymous poetess who wrote, before being put to death in Auschwitz:

> There is no more hope in the white skull
> Among the barbed wire, under the ruins,
> And our dust is scattered in the dust
> Out of the broken jars . . .
> Our army will go forth, skullbone and jawbone,
> And bone to bone, a merciless line,
> We, the hunted who hunt, will cry to you:
> The murdered demand justice at your hands!

TESTIMONY FROM THE NUREMBERG TRIALS

Document Number R-91 is Exhibit USA-241. This document consists of a communication dated the 16th day of December, 1942, sent by Müller to Himmler, for the Chief of the Security Police and SD, and deals with the seizure of Polish Jews for deportation to concentration camps in Germany. I am beginning with the first paragraph. It says, quoting directly:

"In connection with the increase in the transfer of labor to the concentration camps ordered to be completed by 30 January, 1943, the following procedure may be applied in the Jewish section:

"1. Total number: 45,000 Jews.

"2. Start of transportation: 11 January 1943. End of transportation: 31 January 1943. (The Reich railroads are unable to provide special trains for the evacuation during the period from 15 December 1942 to 10 January 1943 because of the increased traffic of Armed Forces leave trains.)

"3. Composition: The 45,000 Jews are to consist of 30,000 Jews from the district of Bialystok; 10,000 Jews from the Ghetto of Theresienstadt, 5,000 of whom are Jews fit for work who heretofore had been used for smaller jobs required for the ghetto and 5,000 Jews who are generally incapable of working, also Jews over 60 years old."

ELEVEN

Jewish Resistance

The horrors of the Holocaust were impossible to believe, even for those who lived through them. The hopes of emancipation, the promise of the future were long since extinguished, but along with the horror came moments of resistance. At first, the Jews could not believe that they were being exterminated, murdered in cold blood. When the truth was undeniable, many fought back. The Warsaw ghetto uprising of 1943 is the best known and documented of these revolts. Below are a description of the Warsaw ghetto uprising, a manifesto of Jewish resistance from the lesser-known revolt in the Vilna ghetto, and the last letter of Mordecai Anilewicz, leader of the Warsaw revolt.

WARSAW GHETTO REVOLT

Life in the ghetto during that week is difficult to describe. I had lived in the ghetto for years. Jews were waiting, they were embracing and kissing during the first days. And although it was clear to every one of us that we should not survive, there was this feeling that Jews had lived to avenge their brethren. But there is no revenge. We fought for our lives; we fought back. That made it easier to die.

I remember the second day of this uprising—this was Pessah. In one of the bunkers I met a Rabbi, Rabbi Meisel. We, the underground, had connections with him also on ordinary days. The underground was not always helped and encouraged by Jews. We were not always well received. Some of them thought we harmed the Jewish community. There was the sense of responsibility which the Germans' terror had succeeded in instilling. When I came into the bunker, the Rabbi stopped the ceremony of the Seder and said, "You are welcome. I die a happier man now. I wish we had done this earlier."

And thus the fighting continued for days. From the very first day we were looking for contacts with the "Aryan" side. We had a number of friends on the "Aryan" side, whom I knew. Yitzhak Zuckerman was our representative there, maintaining contact with the Polish underground, with a view to securing arms. After some time he did succeed in getting hold of arms. But the question was how to smuggle the arms into the ghetto. At that time we had telephone communication besides contact through the men of the *Hevra Kadisha* (Burial Society)—our cemetery was not within the ghetto walls, and since the men of the *Hevra Kadisha* were overworked they always had to leave the ghetto and come back, and so we received arms. We received news from Zuckerman that he had got hold of a number of guns which would be smuggled in within a few days. We also sent letters outside the ghetto through those men in the burial unit, and we sent a letter from Mordecai Anilewicz. And then this contact was also stopped.

We began looking for ways and means to send out a number of comrades—we had very few on the "Aryan" side. I was ordered to inspect this bunker. The ghetto was surrounded all the time by German sentries and artillery, and every movement in the ghetto, the rustling of a leaf, would draw a volley of shots. The approach to the house was difficult. But we did reach that house. We found a bunker, full of food, and there was a way out to the "Aryan" side.

Besides the Jewish Fighting organizations which included all the Jewish youth from right to left, there was a Revisionist group in Muranow Street, and they had prepared this exit a few days before after difficult and brave fighting, and decided to cross over to the "Aryan" side. We met one of them later, and he told us the story. They were all captured and killed.

We, through this same exit and without knowing this story, sent two comrades to establish contact with our comrades on the "Aryan" side—Simha Rathieser, now in Jerusalem, and another comrade who is dead. When they came to the "Aryan" side, a Polish sentry saw them, and believing they were Poles, said, "Do you know what happened here an hour ago?," and he told them about the fighting which had taken place just an hour before. The place was full of Germans and no one was allowed in or out of the place. Yet their courage, maybe their good fortune, helped them to evade the German guards and to contact Yitzhak. They were an important reinforcement to this small group many of whom were killed during the first days of our fight on the "Aryan" side. They helped to evacuate the fighters, and assisted in all underground activities which continued until the liberation.

The Germans could not defeat us in open battle, so they adopted other tactics. Certainly to fight fires was quite impossible. They did not have to fight us because the fire fought us.

(From evidence by Zivia Lubetkin at Eichmann Trial, reprinted in Tzur and Yavnai, eds., *The Holocaust*)

A MANIFESTO: JEWISH RESISTANCE IN VILNA

Offer armed resistance! Jews, defend yourselves with arms!

The German and Lithuanian executioners are at the gates of the ghetto. They have come to murder us! Soon they will lead you forth in groups through the ghetto door.

In the same way they carried away hundreds of us on the day of Yom Kippur. In the same way those with white, yellow and pink *Schein** were deported during the night. In this way our brothers, sisters, mothers, fathers, and sons were taken away.

*Safe conduct passes. To deceive and bewilder the Jews, the Germans constantly changed the colors of the passes which were to have safeguarded them against deportation, always further limiting the number of persons entitled to them.

Tens of thousands of us were dispatched. But we shall not go! We will not offer our heads to the butcher like sheep.

Jews, defend yourselves with arms!

Do not believe the false promises of the assassins or believe the words of the traitors.

Anyone who passes through the ghetto gate will go to Ponar!

And Ponar means death!

Jews, we have nothing to lose. Death will overtake us in any event. And who can still believe in survival when the murderer exterminates us with so much determination? The hand of the executioner will reach each man and woman. Flight and acts of cowardice will not save our lives.

Active resistance alone can save our lives and our honor.

Brothers! It is better to die in battle in the ghetto than to be carried away to Ponar like sheep. And know this: Within the walls of the ghetto there are organized Jewish forces who will resist with weapons.

Support the revolt!

Do not take refuge or hide in the bunkers, for then you will fall into the hands of the murderers like rats.

Jewish people, go out into the squares. Anyone who has no weapons should take an ax, and he who has no ax should take a crowbar or a bludgeon!

For our ancestors!

For our murdered children!

Avenge Ponar!

Attack the murderers!

In every street, in every courtyard, in every house within and without the ghetto, attack these dogs!

Jews, we have nothing to lose! We shall save our lives only if we exterminate our assassins.

Long live liberty! Long live armed resistance! Death to the assassins!

The Commander of the F.P.A.
Vilna, the Ghetto: September 1, 1943.

(From Glatstein, *et al.*, eds., *Anthology of Holocaust Literature*)

MORDECAI ANILEWICZ'S LAST LETTER

It is now clear to me that what took place exceeded all expectations. In our opposition to the Germans we did more than our strength allowed—but now our forces are waning. We are on the brink of extinction. We forced the Germans to retreat twice—but they returned stronger than before.

One of our groups held out for forty minutes; and another fought for about six hours. The mine which was laid in the area of the brush factory exploded as planned. Then we attacked the Germans and they suffered heavy casualties. Our losses were generally low. That is an accomplishment too. Z. fell, next to his machine-gun.

I feel that great things are happening and that this action which we have dared to take is of enormous value.

We have no choice but to go over to partisan methods of fighting as of today. Tonight, six fighting-groups are going out. They have two tasks—to reconnoitre the area and to capture weapons. Remember, "short-range weapons" are of no use to us. We employ them very rarely. We need many rifles, hand-grenades, machine-guns and explosives.

I cannot describe the conditions in which the Jews of the Ghetto are now "living." Only a few exceptional individuals will be able to survive such suffering. The others will sooner or later die. Their fate is certain, even though thousands are trying to hide in cracks and rat holes. It is impossible to light a candle, for lack of air. Greetings to you who are outside. Perhaps a miracle will occur and we shall see each other again one of these days. It is extremely doubtful.

The last wish of my life has been fulfilled. Jewish self-defense has become a fact. Jewish resistance and revenge have become actualities. I am happy to have been one of the first Jewish fighters in the ghetto.

Where will rescue come from?

Mordecai Anilewicz
Warsaw: During the Revolt, 1943.

(From Glatstein *et al.*, eds., *Anthology of Holocaust Literature*)

TWELVE

War Trials

With the defeat of Nazi Germany, the Holocaust ended. It was not just another war. The discovery of the extent of the German atrocities moved the world powers into a re-evaluation of international moral law. Two major war trials resulted. The first, the Nuremberg Trials, were conducted by the Allies immediately after the war. The second, which took place in Jerusalem in 1961, was of Adolf Eichmann, for crimes committed against humanity. The Eichmann trial was the first such trial by a sovereign Jewish state, and served as an international reminder of the Holocaust. Both trials represent the attempt of the civilized world to come to terms with the horrors of Nazi inhumanity.

Here is the brief and explicit executive order issued by President Harry S Truman on May 2, 1945 providing for United States participation in the Nuremberg tribunal:

> EXECUTIVE ORDER 9547: Providing for Representation of the United States in Preparing and Prosecuting Charges of Atrocities and War Crimes Against the Leaders of the European Axis Powers and Their Principal Agents and Accessories.
>
> By virtue of the authority vested in me as President and

as Commander in Chief of the Army and Navy, under the Constitution and statutes of the United States, it is ordered as follows:

1. Associate Justice Robert H. Jackson is hereby designated to act as the Representative of the United States and as its Chief of Counsel in preparing and prosecuting charges of atrocities and war crimes against such of the leaders of the European Axis powers and their principal agents and accessories as the United States may agree with any of the United Nations to bring to trial before an international military tribunal. He shall serve without additional compensation, but shall receive such allowance for expenses as may be authorized by the President.

2. The Representative named herein is authorized to select and recommend to the President or to the head of any executive department, independent establishment, or other federal agency necessary personnel to assist in the performance of his duties hereunder. The head of each executive department, independent establishment, and other federal agency is hereby authorized to assist the Representative named herein in the performance of his duties hereunder and to employ such personnel and make such expenditures, within the limits of appropriations now and hereafter available for the purpose, as the Representative named herein may deem necessary to accomplish the purposes of this order, and may make available, assign, or detail for duty with the Representative named herein such members of the armed forces and other personnel as may be requested for such purposes.

3. The Representative named herein is authorized to cooperate with, and receive the assistance of, any foreign Government to the extent deemed necessary by him to accomplish the purposes of this order.

The White House *Harry S Truman*
May 2, 1945

This executive order was followed by an agreement and a charter of the Allies in which they, too, clearly defined the need for such an undertaking and the procedures under which it was to be conducted.

AGREEMENT: AUGUST 8, 1945

AGREEMENT by the Government of the United States of America, the Provisional Government of the French Republic, the Government of the United Kingdom of Great Britain and Northern Ireland and the Government of the Union of Soviet Socialist Republics for the Prosecution and Punishment of the Major War Criminals of the European Axis.

Whereas the United Nations have from time to time made declarations of their intention that War Criminals shall be brought to justice;

And whereas the Moscow Declaration of the 30th October 1943 on German atrocities in Occupied Europe stated that those German Officers and men and members of the Nazi Party who have been responsible for or have taken a consenting part in atrocities and crimes will be sent back to the countries in which their abominable deeds were done in order that they may be judged and punished according to the laws of these liberated countries and of the free governments that will be created therein;

And whereas this Declaration was stated to be without prejudice to the case of major criminals whose offenses have no particular geographical location and who will be punished by the joint decision of the Governments of the Allies;

Now therefore the Government of the United States of America, the Provisional Government of the French Republic, the Government of the United Kingdom of Great Britain and Northern Ireland and the Government of the Union of Soviet Socialist Republics (hereinafter called "the Signatories") acting in the interests of all the United Nations and by their representatives duly authorized thereto have concluded this Agreement.

Article 1. There shall be established after consultation with the Control Council for Germany an International Military Tribunal for the trial of war criminals whose offenses have no particular geographical location whether they be accused individually or in their capacity as members of organizations or groups or in both capacities.

Article 2. The constitution, jurisdiction and functions of the International Military Tribunal shall be those set out in the Charter annexed to this Agreement, which Charter shall form an integral part of this Agreement.

Article 3. Each of the Signatories shall take the necessary steps to make available for the investigation of the charges and trial the major war criminals detained by them who are to be tried by the International Military Tribunal. The Signatories shall also use their best endeavors to make available for investigation of the charges against and the trial before the International Military Tribunal such of the major war criminals as are not in the territories of any of the Signatories.

Article 4. Nothing in this Agreement shall prejudice the provisions established by the Moscow Declaration concerning the return of war criminals to the countries where they committed their crimes.

Article 5. Any Government of the United Nations may adhere to this Agreement by notice given through the diplomatic channel to the Government of the United Kingdom, who shall inform the other signatory and adhering Governments of each such adherence.

Article 6. Nothing in this Agreement shall prejudice the jurisdiction or the powers of any national or occupation court established or to be established in any allied territory or in Germany for the trial of war criminals.

Article 7. This Agreement shall come into force on the day of signature and shall remain in force for the period of one year and shall continue thereafter, subject to the right of any Signatory to give, through the diplomatic channel, one month's notice of intention to terminate it. Such termination shall not prejudice any proceedings already taken or any findings already made in pursuance of this Agreement.

In witness whereof the Undersigned have signed the present Agreement.

Done in quadruplicate in London this 8th day of August 1945 each in English, French, and Russian, and each text to have equal authenticity.

For the Government of the United States of America
Robert H. Jackson
For the Provisional Government of the French Republic
Robert Falco
For the Government of the
United Kingdom of Great Britain and Northern Ireland
C. Jowitt
For the Government of the Union of Soviet Socialist Republics
I. Nikitchenko, A. Trainin

CHARTER: AUGUST 8, 1945

Article 5. In case of need and depending on the number of the matters to be tried, other Tribunals may be set up; and the establishment, functions, and procedure of each Tribunal shall be identical, and shall be governed by this Charter.

II. Jurisdiction and General Principles

Article 6. The Tribunal established by the Agreement referred to in Article 1 hereof for the trial and punishment of the major war criminals of the European Axis countries shall have the power to try and punish persons who, acting in the interests of the European Axis countries, whether as individuals or as members of organizations, committed any of the following crimes.

The following acts, or any of them, are crimes coming within the jurisdiction of the Tribunal for which there shall be individual responsibility:

(a) Crimes Against Peace: namely, planning, preparation, initiation or waging of a war of aggression, or a war in violation of international treaties, agreements or assurances, or participation in a common plan or conspiracy for the accomplishment of any of the foregoing;

(b) War Crimes: namely, violations of the laws or customs of war. Such violations shall include, but not be limited to, murder, ill-treatment or deportation to slave labor or for any other purpose of civilian population of or in occupied territory, murder or ill-treatment of prisoners of war or persons on the seas, killing of hostages, plunder of public or private property, wanton destruction of cities, towns, or villages, or devastation not justified by military necessity;

(c) Crimes Against Humanity: namely, murder, extermination, enslavement, deportation, and other inhumane acts committed against any civilian populace, before or during the war; or persecutions on political, racial or religious grounds in execution of or in connection with any crime within the jurisdiction of the Tribunal, whether or not in violation of the domestic law of the country where perpetrated.

Leaders, organizers, instigators, and accomplices participating in the formulation or execution of a common plan or conspiracy to commit any of the foregoing crimes are responsible for all acts performed by any persons in execution of such plan.

A full report on the unprecedented Nuremberg Trials was sent to President Harry S Truman by Mr. Justice Jackson. This selection is presented as a summary. In it Jackson expresses his personal hope that these trials would be a moral force in preventing "man's inhumanity to man."

REPORT TO THE PRESIDENT
BY MR. JUSTICE JACKSON

October 7, 1946

The President
The White House
Washington, D.C.

My Dear Mr. President:

I have the honor to report as to the duties which you delegated to me on May 2, 1945 in connection with the prosecution of major Nazi war criminals.

The International Military Tribunal sitting at Nuremberg, Germany on 30 September and 1 October, 1946 rendered judgment in the first international criminal assizes in history. It found 19 of the 22 defendants guilty on one or more of the counts of the Indictment, and acquitted 3. It sentenced 12 to death by hanging, 3 to imprisonment for life, and the four others to terms of 10 to 20 years imprisonment.

The Tribunal also declared 4 Nazi organizations to have been criminal in character. These are: The Leadership Corps of the Nazi Party; *Die Schutzstaffeln,* known as the SS; *Die Sicherheitsdienst,* known as the SD; and *Die Geheimstaatspolizei,* known as the Gestapo, or Secret State Police. It declined to make that finding as to *Die Sturmabteilungen,* known as the SA; the *Reichscabinet,* and the General Staff and High Command. The latter was solely because the structure of the particular group was considered by the Tribunal to be too loose to constitute a coherent "group" or "organization," and was not because of any doubt of its criminality in war plotting. In its judgment the Tribunal condemned the officers who performed General Staff and High Command functions as "a ruthless military caste" and said they were "responsible in large measure for the miseries and suffering that have fallen on millions of men, women and children. They have been a disgrace to the honorable profession of arms." This finding should dispose of any fear that we were prosecuting soldiers just because they fought for their country and lost, but the failure to hold the General Staff to be a criminal organization is regrettable.

The magnitude of the task which, with this judgment, has been brought to conclusion may be suggested statistically: The trial began on November 20, 1945 and occupied 216 days of trial time. 33 witnesses were called and examined for the prosecution. 61 witnesses and 19 defendants testified for the defense; 143 additional witnesses gave testimony by interrogatories for the defense. The proceedings were conducted and recorded in four languages—English, German, French, and Russian—and daily transcripts in the language of his choice was provided for each prosecuting staff and all counsel for defendants. The English transcript of the proceedings covers over 17,000 pages. All proceedings were sound-reported in the original language used.

In preparation for the trial over 100,000 captured German documents were screened or examined and about 10,000 were selected for intensive examination as having probable evidentiary value. Of these, about 4,000 were translated into four languages and used, in whole or in part, in the trial as exhibits. Millions of feet of captured moving picture film were examined and over 100,000 feet brought to Nuremberg. Relevant sections were prepared and introduced as exhibits. Over 25,000 captured still photographs were brought to Nuremberg, together with Hitler's personal photographer who took most of them. More than 1,800 were selected and prepared for use as exhibits. The Tribunal, in its judgment, states: "The case, therefore, against the defendants rests in large measure on documents of their own making, the authenticity of which has not been challenged except in one or two cases." The English translations of most of the documents are now being published by the Department of State and War in eight volumes and will be a valuable and permanent source for the war history. As soon as funds are available, additional volumes will be published so that the entire documentary aspect of the trial—prosecution and defense—will be readily available....

...I hereby resign my commission as your representative and Chief Counsel for the United States. In its execution I have had the help of many able men and women, too many to mention individually, who have made personal sacrifice to carry on a work in which they earnestly believed. I also want to express deep personal appreciation for this opportunity to do what I believe to be a constructive work for the peace of the world and for the better protection of persecuted peoples. It was, perhaps, the greatest opportunity ever presented to an American lawyer. In pursuit of it many mistakes have been made and many inadequacies must be confessed. I am consoled by the fact that in proceedings of this novelty, errors and missteps may also be instructive to the future.

> Respectfully submitted,
> [sig.] *Robert H. Jackson*

The Nuremberg Trials were the first of a succession involving Nazi war criminals. Of special significance was the Eichmann trial, held in Jerusalem, the capital of the Jewish State. It was formally convened as a court of justice with the rights of the defendant clearly protected.

Eichmann had been pursued after his escape at the end of the war, and was finally found living in Buenos Aires, Argentina. He was captured and brought to Israel by the Israeli secret service.

Eichmann, like so many escaped war criminals, was tracked down by Simon Wiesenthal, a concentration camp survivor, who has dedicated himself to the capture and conviction of these "murderers among us."

This selection of testimony, taken from the records of the Nuremberg trials, gives us some idea of the nature and magnitude of Eichmann's crimes.

TESTIMONY FROM THE NUREMBERG TRIALS

The Jews of Hungary suffered the same tragic fate. Between 19 March 1944 and the 1st of August 1944, more than 400,000 Hungarian Jews were rounded up. Many of these were put in wagons and sent to extermination camps, and we refer to Document Number 2605-PS, Exhibit USA-242. This document is an affidavit made in London by Dr. Rudolph Kastner, a former official of the Hungarian Zionist Organization. We refer to page 3 of the document, the third full paragraph. In March 1944, quoting:

"Together with the German military occupation, there arrived in Budapest a 'Special Section Commando' of the German Secret Police with the sole object of liquidating the Hungarian Jews. It was headed by Adolf Eichmann, SS Obersturmbannführer, Chief of Section IV B of the Reich Security Head Office. His immediate collaborators were: SS Obersturmbannführer Herman Krumey, Hauptsturmführer Wisliczeny, Hunsche, Novak, Dr. Weidl, and later Danegger, Wrtok. They arrived and later deported to Mauthausen all the leaders of Jewish political and business life and journalists, together with the Hungarian democratic and anti-fascist politicians; taking advantage of the 'interregnum' following upon the German occupation lasting 4 days, they have placed their Quislings in the Ministry of the Interior."

On Page 7 of that same document, the 8th paragraph, beginning with the words "Commanders of the death camps" and quoting:

"Commanders of the death camps gassed only on direct or indirect instructions of Eichmann. The particular officer of IV B who directed the deportations from some particular country had the authority to indicate whether the train should go to a death camp or not and what should happen to the passengers. The instructions were usually carried by the SS non-commissioned officers escorting the train. The letters 'A' or 'M'—capital letters 'A' or 'M'—on the escorting instruction documents indicated Auschwitz (Oswieczim) or Majdanek; it meant that the passengers were to be gassed."

Simon Wiesenthal's description of Eichmann adds a human perspective to these inhuman crimes.

EICHMANN, THE ELUSIVE

I saw Adolf Eichmann for the first time the opening day of his trial in the courtroom in Jerusalem. For nearly sixteen years I had thought of him practically every day and every night. In my mind I had built up the image of a demonic superman. Instead I saw a frail, nondescript, shabby fellow in a glass cell between two Israeli policemen; they looked more colorful and interesting than he did. Everything about Eichmann seemed drawn with charcoal; his grayish face, his balding head, his clothes. There was nothing demonic about him; he looked like a bookkeeper who is afraid to ask for a raise. Something seemed completely wrong, and I kept thinking about it while the incomprehensible bill of indictment ("the murder of six million men, women, and children") was being read. Suddenly I knew what it was. In my mind I'd always seen SS Obersturmbannführer Eichmann, supreme arbiter of life and death. But the Eichmann I now saw did not wear the SS uniform of terror and murder. Dressed in a cheap, dark suit, he seemed a cardboard figure, empty and two-dimensional. Later I told First Procurator Hausner that Eichmann should have worn a uniform. That would have re-created the real identity and true image of the Eichmann the witnesses remembered. They, too, seemed a little puzzled by the shabby little civilian in the glass cell. Hausner said that emotionally I was right but that the idea was not practical. It might have given the aura of a show trial, a masquerade. The Israelis were aware that they had been under the continuous scrutiny of the whole world since they had captured Eichmann and brought him across the ocean, and they wanted to avoid unnecessary criticism. I had one other suggestion, also obviously impractical. Fifteen times, after each item of the indictment, Eichmann was asked whether he was guilty. Each time, he said "Not guilty." This procedure, too, seemed inadequate to me. I thought that Eichmann should have been asked six million times, and he should have been made to answer six million times.

By committing the perfectly incredible crime, the Nazis had hoped to get away with it before the bar of history. Future generations wouldn't believe that such a thing could have happened. Ergo, the Nazis deduced, history would one day conclude that it had not happened. The crime was of such a scope that it was inconceivable.

After weeks in the courtroom I was oppressed by a growing sense of unreality. The courtroom was a gloomy, fortified island in the busy, sunlit city of Jerusalem. The island was guarded by soldiers with submachine guns. The spectators were searched for weapons. When I left this fortress of retribution and walked out into the sun of Israel, children were playing in the street, people were coming home from work, young couples were in love, women carried shopping bags. They seemed totally unaware of the tragedy that was being recalled in the courtroom. I remember being annoyed about the seeming indifference of these people, but I know it was absurd to blame them; almost all of them had lost a relative or a friend because of the little man in the glass cell. Life went on; life was stronger than the defendant in the courtroom, with the forest of six million dead behind him.

Eichmann's capture came at the right moment psychologically. Had he been caught at the end of the war and tried in Nuremberg, his crimes might now be forgotten. He would have been only another face among the defendants in the dock. At that time, everybody was glad that the nightmare was over. Until the trial of Eichmann, there were millions of people in Germany and Austria who pretended not to know or didn't want to know about the enormity of the SS crimes. The trial did away with such self-deception; after it, no one could claim ignorance. Eichmann, the man, didn't count. He was dead the moment he entered the courtroom. But millions of people read about him, heard the story of the "Final Solution" on radio, and saw the courtroom drama on the television screen. They heard Eichmann's colorless voice, saw his impassive face. Only once did he come close to something resembling emotion, on the ninety-fifth day of the trial, when he said: "I must admit that I now consider the annihilation of the Jews one of the worst crimes in the history of mankind. But it did happen, and we must do all we can to prevent it from happening again."

I've since talked to many Germans and Austrians about the trial. Almost all of them were impressed by the judicial procedure. They realized that the incredible crime had happened. They had to re-examine their consciences.

And perhaps some of them came to the same conclusion as Eichmann—it must never happen again.

The Eichmann trial proved the inadequacy of human law. The criminal codes of all civilized nations know the definition of murder. The lawmakers were thinking of the murder of one person, or two, or fifty, or maybe a thousand persons. But the systematic extermination of six million people blasts the framework of all law. It is like the explosive force of an H bomb—something people don't want to think of. Eichmann understood this very well. In Budapest he said to some friends in 1944: "One hundred dead is a catastrophe. Five million dead is a statistic."

As an architect I learned to build houses according to certain structural rules. I knew that my houses would not withstand an earthquake above a certain force. The "Final Solution of the Jewish Question" was the kind of earthquake for which there were no building rules.

Nearly everything about Eichmann remains incomprehensible. I spent years searching his personal history to find something that might explain why he became what he was. I didn't find anything. Eichmann came from a religious, quiet family. His father, a member of the Presbyterian church, once spoke as the guest of honor at the synagogue in Linz, when the head of the Jewish Community there, Benedikt Schwäger, was awarded a high Austrian decoration.

Unlike Hitler, Eichmann had no unpleasant experiences with Jews. He was not jilted by a Jewish girl or swindled by a Jewish merchant. He was probably honest when he said, at the trial, that he'd only done his job. He said he wouldn't have hesitated to send his own father into a gas chamber if he'd been ordered to do so. Eichmann's great strength was that he treated the Jewish problem unemotionally. He was the most dangerous man of all—a man with no human feeling. He once said he was not an anti-Semite. But he certainly was antihuman.

Late in April 1945, Eichmann was with the Jewish Council members in Theresienstadt concentration camp, when he saw Rabbi Leo Baeck, one of the leaders of modern Jewry, walk by. Eichmann said he was surprised that Rabbi Baeck was still alive. No one said a word; everybody was afraid Eichmann might issue an order sending Baeck to his death. But Eichmann was in a benevolent mood that day, and he did nothing about Rabbi Baeck. However, as he took his leave, he said amiably to the Jews around him: "Let me tell you something. Jewish death lists are my favorite reading matter before I go to sleep."

He took a few of the lists from the table and walked out.

(From Simon Wiesenthal, *The Murderers Among Us*)

THIRTEEN

Feelings

Materials relating to the Holocaust sources reveal great complexity as well as deep feelings. Included in this section are poems written by Holocaust victims who have left us this eternal legacy. They serve as a marked contrast to the documents and letters, even to the passionate speeches presented thus far. These poems speak to us directly, their content is explicit, their message everlasting.

The very last selection was written by a survivor, Donia Rosen, who, as a child, was rescued from the fires of the Holocaust. It attests to yet another aspect of this period. Donia Rosen's rescuers were people who lived simply, but who became living models for human goodness and nobility. The tragedy of the Holocaust was real, and its horror cannot be exaggerated, but the rare moments of real humanity occasionally shone through and deserve to be mentioned.

SELECTED POEMS

"The Lonely Child" (Dos Elnteh Kind)

> Memories of you
> Are made of despair,
> Oh mama, my mameleh,
> Where are you, where?

Your Sara keeps looking,
Her grief unconcealed . . .
Wandering, lamenting,
Like wind in the field.

Father's not here—
Oh, where can he be?
He was taken away
By a vicious decree.
It was dark on that night
That I cannot erase,
But darker than night
Was my mother's sweet face.

Numb through the day,
Tormented at night,
The unrest of sleep
Brings my papa to sight.
I imagine he's speaking
And walking nearby,
Mama's rocking and singing
This sad lullaby.

Someday you'll be
A mother like me.
You must tell your children
Of our misery:
That your mama and papa
Have suffered this way.
Forget not our yesterday—
Remember it today!

(S. Katcherginski
Translated by J. Eisner and R. Shusterman)

"A Jewish Child" (A Yiddish Kind)

In a village far away
In a room that's damp and gray,
Through the glass, with eyes so wide,
Children peer and gaze outside.
Boys with flaxen heads of gold,
Girls with braids of marigold;
And there among them, but not quite,
Two round eyes of deepest night.

Two black eyes so deep and warm,
A nose of tiny perfect form,
Two sweet lips beyond compare,
Strong and curly, thick black hair;
Here, his mother, full of fright
Brought her only child one night.
How she kissed him as she cried
And gently pressed him to her side.

"Here, my child, is where you'll stay.
Listen, and do what I say.
I must leave you, I must go—
They'll take good care of you, I know.
With the other children, play;
Be polite, don't disobey.
Don't speak a Yiddish word or song—
No more to Jews do you belong."

His arms around his mother flew,
"Oh, Mama, let me go with you.
Mama, don't leave me alone,
Mama, I beg you, not alone!"
She kissed his face, his swollen eyes,
Still, that would not stop his cries.
Once again, "No, Mama no,
Don't make me stay here all alone."

In her arms she holds her child,
And with a voice so sweet and mild
She sings, she croons, but does not weep,
Rocks him till he falls asleep.
Now she cries with all her heart
But she knows she must depart.
Full of worry, grief and fright,
Out she stumbles to the night.

The night is cold, the wind is wild,
A voice is sobbing, "Oh, my child!
I left you in a stranger's hand,
What else could I do—please understand!"
No one hears her, only fate,
And outside, it's cold and late.
The night is cold, the wind is wild,
"Please, God—protect my only child!"

The room is strange, the people, too,
He's always mute, the little Jew.
He doesn't ask a single thing,
Never does he smile or sing.
Day or night, he cannot feel,
His life is dead, he cannot heal.
Vasilka—a strange new name.
Vasilka—it brings him pain.

The mother wanders where she will.
Like her Yoseleh, she's still.
No one's bothered by her fate,
She can only wait and wait.
Like Jocheved, Israel's daughter,
Her son, like Moses, on the water,
Serious, sad, alone, aggrieved,
She's lost the child that she conceived.

(Chaneh Chaitin
Translated by J. Eisner and R. Shusterman)

"Twilight in the Children's Sick Room"

The last light of day has lingered long enough
And now the twilight softly steals
Into the children's sick room—
Casts its magic glow upon the little beds
And tenderly caresses the fever-flushed cheeks.
This is the hour of stories and make-believe,
And wistful whispers fill the lonely room.

"I had a dream
that I was in the land of milk and honey,"
speaks a little voice beneath a bandaged head.
"And in my dream
I sat for hours underneath a tree
and ate and ate and ate."

"What did you eat?" demands his little neighbor,
and she lifts her head up from her musty pillow.

"Cakes, sausage—all sorts of things—
What one usually eats in the land of milk and honey."

"Oh, cakes," reminisces another child
who for months has felt nothing but hunger.
"I wish I had a mashed potato ... "

"And I," another little voice calls out,
"how I would love an egg!"

The memory of an egg
Finds a chorus
Which is echoed through the room
As all agree how good an egg would be.

"We had an apple tree at home.
I wish I had an apple from there."

From the corner of the room
Where tuberculosis patients stay,
Little Heinz, with cheek so pale that
Fine blue veins now mottle the transparent skin, says,
"If only I could have
What I used to leave behind on my own plate.
Once upon a time I didn't like
Hot soup or meat or hash.
There used to be a fight at every meal . . .
Now mother is dying and father is dead
And I am longing for a crust of dry bread."

"My uncle once brought me a gingerbread man!"
boasts Evi as she laughs aloud.

Peterleh dreamily gazes at nothing.
"Chocolate, chocolate,
do you remember the sweet taste of chocolate?"

"Oh, go on with your gingerbread men and your candy!
What I'd like is real food like green beans and peas
in portions so big that I never would find
the bottom of the plate."

"Yes!" interrupts little Lise with glee,
"I'd like lots of vegetables!
Spinach and cabbage, potatoes and eggplant—
I wouldn't mind even eating them raw!"

The chatter goes on through the hour of twilight
And now it is evening and time for their meal.
I turn on the light and my heart shrinks with pain
The glare of the bulb brings an end to their talk.
For dinner there's coffee, black and unsweetened.

(Ilse Weber: Theresienstadt
Translated by J. Eisner and R. Shusterman)

"The Grabber's Prayer" (Di Tfileh fun Chapper)

My body burns with emptiness
And hunger is my father,
A ghetto-chapper am I now,
A robber, starred in yellow.

A wagon comes at break of day
With fresh bread from the oven;
My heart is choked, my need so great,
My eyes are wet with hunger.

So hear me, God in heaven above,
So hear me, God, my dear one,
I want to get my share of life
But God, I need to eat.
So give me fingers quick as light
And eyes as bright as fire.

I grab, I'm beaten for the bread,
But whips and sticks can't hurt me.
What's life to me, what's death to me?
There's nothing left to scare me.

Here comes a couple down the street.
It's night—no one can see me.
A jump, a grab, and then they scream—
Too late—my teeth have bitten.

I thank you, God, for every night
That you have given man,
For while they sleep, my day begins,
A life of ghetto-thieving.

So hear me, God, forgive my sin,
So hear me, God, my dear one.
The world has pushed me from your laws,
I didn't mean to stray,
A ghetto thief, an outcast now,
Between two worlds I linger.

(Irene Geisler: Warsaw Ghetto
Translated by J. Eisner and R. Shusterman)

Memoirs of Humanity

I set out alone. No one paid any attention to me as I walked along. Over my shoulder I carried a sack of apples. When I reached the vicinity of the old nest I hid in the forest. Then, during the night, I stole into the little cottage where Olena waited for me. Stefan believed that I was not living in the house, but apparently he did retain some doubts. Since he was a frequent visitor at the cottage it was very difficult to hide from him. Then, as though maliciously, he began to come even more often. He was not looking for me particularly, but he would look into every corner suspiciously. There was a time when I had believed that this man would help me; now he had become a nightmare. I had to hide from him, too. Whenever I heard him approach the house, jingling the keys in his hand, I would hide under the stove, sliding into my hiding place like a frightened mouse and lying there quietly. One day I slipped under the stove, as usual with Stefan in the house, but he just kept sitting there. He sat as though he had no intention of ever leaving. I began to feel that I simply could not lie there in that dark corner any longer. I moved slightly. It is unlikely that he would have heard me under normal conditions, but this time, his senses sharpened by fear, he heard even the slight rustle I made. He walked over to my hiding place and ordered me to come out. I obeyed and stood dumb, waiting for what was to come.

"What is the big idea?" he demanded in controlled tones, as though forcing himself to be somewhat polite.

"I have no intention of disturbing you; I expect no help from you," I said. "You are one of those people I'm hiding from."

He looked at me angrily and quickly left the house. The sound of the key turning in the lock frightened me and I didn't budge until Olena returned. I told her what had happened and we discussed the new situation at length, finally deciding that the only thing I could do was to remain in the cottage despite what had happened.

Stefan did not show up again. Frightening days passed. Olena continued to work and I benefitted from her compassion and her good heart and remained alive. Sometimes she would bring home a worn page of an old newspaper, or a tattered book. I was afraid to think of the future. I could not imagine that I would last out the war, and as for after the war—the very concept had no meaning for me. The Jews of Europe will not survive this war, I thought, and nightmares remained my constant companions.

On the night of the tenth of December, 1942, Olena had not returned home although it was already quite late.

I was terrified. A wild, branch-breaking snowstorm raged outside. The windows of the little cottage were sealed with snow and the cottage itself swayed like a drunkard. The howling of the wind was like a siren, warning of new terrors. Within the room it was frighteningly quiet, with even the chirping of the cricket behind the stove stopping from time to time. I waited. With all my might I yearned for the door to open and reveal Olena, my rescuer and savior. The loneliness frightened me and the howling of the wind sounded like the sighs of the dying. In vain I listened for the sound of the familiar footsteps. The raging wind grew stronger, its howling piercing the skies. I huddled up to the stove, looking for protection. Perhaps something had happened to her, I thought. It was very late when the door finally opened and Olena appeared. She was covered with snow, which began to melt very quickly and drip from her clothing onto the floor. The old woman could barely catch her breath, and she sank into a chair, exhausted. She had battled the storm, and made it home only with the greatest difficulty. Her eyes darted about the room in fright, and her hands trembled nervously.

"What happened to you, Olena," I asked, my alarm growing. Olena took a deep breath, and stood up. "The Germans have surrounded the village, and they are searching every house looking for Jews. They have already caught three Jewish women and killed one of them. Please, run for your life, run!" Outside, the very foundations of the earth seemed to shake. We set out, into a black, raging void. The wind drove us ahead, tossing us about like dry branches. We kept sinking into the cold whiteness and climbing out again. The snow covered our eyes and our ears. We fell, got up again, walked and fell again, holding hands and battling the storm. To add to the difficulty Olena was carrying a ladder on her shoulder.

Our strength was exhausted but fear kept us moving. We finally reached a huge haystack. I climbed to the top and Olena took the ladder away and left me. It seemed to me that I would very quickly come tumbling down; that the wild wind would topple me along with the haystack. Huge, sticky snowflakes fell and covered me completely. I was soon covered by a mantle of snow, an indistinguishable part of the haystack. I was afraid to move and I lay there for a long time, even though paralyzed by the cold and by fear. The sound of shots, carried by the wind, seemed to be coming closer. The howling of the wind was transformed into a cry of despair. Then, suddenly, I heard footsteps near the haystack. They've tracked me down, I thought; here they come. Fear conjured up terrifying pictures. I was frozen, with no sensation in my hands or feet.

I'll die of the cold, I thought. After a while the cold turned to warmth and I began to doze. I sank into a restful sleep and would certainly have frozen to death had Olena not come back and wakened me.

"Come home," she said. "It's after midnight and I don't think the Germans will come anymore in such a storm." I couldn't walk on my frozen feet, and the old woman dragged me home. The murmur of the fire in the stove filled the room; the warmth caressed me; I could almost feel it with my hands. Outside, the storm still raged; it seemed as though the snow was determined to cover the earth. The window panes rattled and the cottage swayed, making me sleepy. The feeling that I once again had a roof over my head, was wrapped in warmth and back with Olena comforted me.

"Sleep, sleep in peace, my child, the Germans won't come any more, it's late, and the weather is bad," she whispered to me. I relaxed, and began to warm up. I let myself think of tomorrow, of freedom.

Oh, if I could only survive until the war ended. I would embrace the whole world: I would press myself to mother-earth and kiss her. I would fly through the air like a bird–fly endlessly. The forest would murmur once again, and the bells would ring out a song of victory, of redemption, of freedom. The flowers would smile, the grass would rustle with pleasure. All mankind would be good; there would be freedom and the right to live! I dozed off, and my sleep was sweet, full of dreams of a better future.

Suddenly there was the sound of feet stamping in the

snow, and then a violent knocking on the door. At first I thought it was the wind. The pounding came again.

"Olena, we're lost," I said.

"Be quiet, and don't budge," she answered, motioning me to be still. Another knock.

"Who is that knocking on the door, not letting me sleep?" Olena called out loudly.

"Police," came the answer, in a low, rough voice from outside.

Olena opened the door. A German and two neighborhood Ukrainians stood there.

Be damned, you murderers, you sowers of evil. Why doesn't the earth collapse under your feet? Why doesn't the lightning strike you dead? I thought. The snow kept falling; the wind, howling. What was I do do? Where was I to flee? I crawled under the bed, coiled up like a spring, and glued myself to the wall. If I had remained outside just a little longer I might have spared myself this calamity, and now, all was lost. I was overwhelmed by despair. Helplessly, I surrendered to my fate, and waited for the bitter end. The murderers stood on the threshold, with Olena confronting them. Olena, who was threatened by the same danger that threatened me, stood there like a heroine, sure of herself, unmoved. I felt ashamed of myself as I watched her. Michailo Shenkarek spoke to her almost gently:

"As you know, Olena, there is a rumor going round that there are Jews hidden in our village. It is our duty to find them and turn them over to the authorities. It is a shame that there are people among us who are hiding Jews. Your house is remote, on the edge of the village, close to the forest; it would be a good place to hide. And so we ask you, if there is anyone hidden here, turn him over to us. I promise that if you do it willingly you yourself will not be harmed."

"Please, go ahead, you can search: I'm not hiding anyone," Olena answered. She spoke so bravely, with such courage, that my despair vanished and I felt strong enough to carry on. I curled up even more and pressed tightly against the wall.

"So you insist there are no Jews here?"

"There are none."

"We'll look to make sure."

A stream of memories came flowing into my mind. Grandpa and his last plea: *"Ich bitte sie, lassen sie mich leben"*; Salka screaming, "Mommy, I want to live!"; my wounded aunt; Grandma with despair on her face; Kossov dying, but not just Kossov—Kolomiya, Stanislavov, Lvov, Lublin, Lodz, Warsaw ... millions had died! Millions were sacrificed on the altar of evil and brutality.

Why didn't I mount the altar with Grandma, I thought. I could still hear what Werner had said: "My wife has been killed; my children have been killed; tomorrow I will be gone, too. Not one of us will survive."

"Bring a light!" one of them shouted at Olena.

"I am very poor," she answered. "I don't have an oil lamp or even a candle in the house."

"Then how do you live—in the dark?"

"This is the way I live, as you see."

The murderers began to search. They went into the attic, searched and poked around thoroughly, and then came down into the small foyer. They searched with the help of a small battery lamp that was almost exhausted. A small, pale spot of light moved from place to place. They looked into the stove, under the stove, on the bench, and under the bench. They came close to the bed and I could already see them, messengers of death. They must have been deaf, not to hear the pounding of my heart, the dumb scream of despair. The light came close to me and the murderers bent down, searching under the bed. I pressed closer to the wall. I wanted to be completely flat, to shrink, to merge into the wall. I clenched my fists. The spot of light was just centimeters away. I drew my legs up even tighter. The light was still for a moment, and then moved away to the other side.

"There really is no one here," one of them said in surprise, "and I was so sure we would find someone."

They left. I lay there for a long time before I began to come to myself. Outside the snow still fell and the wind howled. I kissed Olena's hands and wept without restraint. I wept for joy, and I wept in sorrow at my lot. I wept without really knowing why. Olena clasped me to her bosom, and said: "We will not give in! Come what may, we will not give in! My own courage grows in the struggle. As long as I remain alive, you will live. It is only now that I feel that my life has any value. At last I feel that someone needs me, that I am living for someone, that I am fighting for something. You have redeemed me from the terrible loneliness, the barrenness, the despair. Don't worry about me. Let me share your fate, your suffering. I want to bear with you to the very end. I am not afraid of death in a battle of my own choosing. I am afraid of a death that brings shame and disgrace; I don't want to die a dog's death among strangers, a useless wanderer, a beggar no one needs. A harsh fate has bound us together and now I cannot imagine life without you."

Olena finally burst into tears. I knew that such friends were rare, not to be traded for gold.

To Olena:

Dear, unforgettable Olena, if I were a sculptress I would make a statue of you. I would perpetuate your exalted image—that of a mother prepared to accept the most brutal suffering for the sake of her children; prepared to give even her life, at any moment. Because you were a mother to me—in place of the mother taken from me at the dawn of my life.

To my sorrow, I am neither sculptress nor poet. I can bring you only this modest tribute—these memoirs, written out of a deep spiritual need. Accept them, dear Olena, as the expression of my deep love for you, an expression of my gratitude and esteem. Dear and beloved Olena—I shall never forget you.

(From Donia Rosen, *The Forest, My Friend*)

For Further Reading

1. Friedlander, Alfred H. *Out of the Whirlwind*: A Reader of Holocaust Literature. New York: Union of American Hebrew Congregations, 1968.

2. Shirer, William L. *The Rise and Fall of the Third Reich*. New York: Simon and Schuster, 1960.

3. Ringelblum, Emmanuel. *Notes From the Warsaw Ghetto*. Edited by and translated by Jacob Sloan. New York: 1958.

4. Hitler, Adolph. *Mein Kampf*. Boston: Houghton Mifflin Co., 1943.

5. Levin, Nora. *The Holocaust*. New York: Thomas Y. Crowell Co., 1968.

6. Morse, Arthur D. *While Six Million Died*. New York: Random House, 1968.

7. Hilberg, Raul. *The Destruction of the European Jews*. Chicago: Quadrangle Books, 1961.

8. _____. *Documents of Destruction*. Chicago: Quadrangle Books, 1971.

9. _____. "German Motivation for the Destruction of the Jews." *Midstream*, June, 1965.

10. Wiesel, Elie. "Words from a Witness." *Conservative Judaism* 21, Volume 3.

11. Ainzstein, Reuben. "They Could Have Been Saved." *The Jewish Spectator*, June, 1967.

12. Mandlin, Oscar. "Jewish Resistance to the Nazis." *Commentary*, 1962.

13. Kaplan, Chaim A. *Scroll of Agony: The Warsaw Diary of Chaim A. Kaplan*. Edited by and translated by Abraham Katsh. New York: Macmillan, 1965.

14. Barbi, Meyer. *The Fighting Ghettos*. Philadelphia: Lippincott, Co., 1962. (First-hand accounts of the Jewish resistance to the Nazis within the ghetto walls, in the concentration camps, and the forests.)

15. Wiesenthal, Simon. *The Murderers Among Us*. New York: McGraw-Hill, 1967.

16. Wiesel, Elie. *Night*. New York: Hill and Wang, 1960.

17. Steiner, Jean Francois. *Treblinka*. New York: Simon and Schuster, Inc., 1967.

18. Rubinstein, Richard. *After Auschwitz*. Indianapolis: The Bobbs-Merrill Co., Inc., 1966.

19. Anatoli, A. (Kuznetsov). *Babi Yar*. New York: Farrar, Straus and Giroux, 1970.

20. Kessel, Sim. *Hanged at Auschwitz*. Translated by Melville and Delight Wallace. New York: Stein and Day, Publishers, 1972.

21. Wiesel, Elie. "The Death Train." From *The World Was Silent*. Translated by Moshe Spiegel. Buenos Aires: Central Farband Fun Poylishe Yidn in Argentina, 1956.

22. Shalit, Levi. "Smugglers." From *This Is How We Died*. Translated from Yiddish by Adah Fogel. Munich: 1949.

23. Landau, Regina. "Bodies of Children for the Animals in the Circus." From *Documents of Crime and Martyrdom*. Translated from Yiddish by Moshe Spiegel. Cracow: Jewish Historical Society of Cracow, 1945.

24. Friedman, Philip. "Jewish Resistance to Nazism." From *European Resistance Movements*, 1939-45. London: Oxford Pergamon Press, 1960.

25. Glatstein, Jacob, Israel Knox, and Samuel Margoshes, eds. *Anthology of Holocaust Literature*. Philadelphia: Jewish Publication Society of America, 1969.

26. *The Holocaust*. Jerusalem: Keter Publishing House, 1974.

A Guide for Discussion

ONE

Emancipation: Demands and Opportunities

The rapid changes in the social order which led to the rise of the modern state also led to a new reality for the Jews. This chapter is used to introduce the concept of the changing social order and its impact on Jewish life. It also demonstrates the tensions which have always existed between the Jews and the majority culture, and could be generalized to consider the relationship of any subgroup to a majority culture. Dohm's essay and the *Acts of the Assembly of Israelitish Deputies of France and Italy* are excellent illustrations of the forces and attitudes which formed the intellectual climate of this period. The keyword "emancipation" indicates the nature of the problem.

Themes

1. Jewish stereotypes in Christian society
   a. Economic
   b. Social
   c. Moral
   d. Religious
   (Themes represented in classic fashion; should be used to study the varied aspects of anti-Jewish attitudes)
2. Anti-Semitism in simplistic terms; multilayered reality spelled out in first readings; indicates the complexity of the problem
3. The nature of the solutions, and how they respond to the issues Dohm raised in the first reading
4. The image of a new social order for all people, and the implicit concept of human nature

Discussion and Activity

1. Discuss the problem of stereotypes in general, and the

problems in dealing with them in society.
2. Find illustrations in contemporary society of these same Jewish stereotypes and attempt to trace their origins in America.
3. Collect stereotypes of other minority groups in literature, newspapers, etc., and discuss their origins, similarities, and contrasts with the Jewish stereotypes.
4. Present social and legal steps which have been attempted for the improvement of these problems. Have they been effective?
5. Discuss the word *emancipation* in this context and in the context of the American slave.

TWO

Late Nineteenth-Century Achievement: Alfred Dreyfus

One approach to the problem of negative stereotypes has been assimilation into the majority culture. Alfred Dreyfus is a classic example of this response.

Themes

1. The identification of the citizen with the state, and not with a religious or ethnic group as a new phenomenon in history
2. Education as a means of achieving integration in the society
3. The selection of the military as a career; the previous reluctance of states to accept Jews into the military as a major theme to be investigated

Discussion and Activity

1. View the film "Zola" for an appreciation of the period.
2. Discuss whether or not self-conscious assimilation is a legitimate tool for the elimination of prejudice. Cite illustrations from contemporary problems.
3. Discuss the lack of Jewish identity on the part of Alfred Dreyfus. Is it self-conscious or is it the result of the process of emancipation explored in Chapter One?

THREE

Late Nineteenth-Century Failure: Alfred Dreyfus

The success or failure of a subgroup to achieve acceptance is never a simple process depending on mere willingness to assimilate. Old stereotypes and the need for scapegoats in times of stress are more often the issues. This chapter points up the existence of complex forces, new and old, contributing to changes in group relations within a society.

Themes

1. The anti-Semitic canard that the Jew is incapable of loyalty to a sovereign nation-state
2. The nature of mass acceptance of a vicious charge and the emotions that result for the individual as seen in the Dreyfus case

Discussion

This is the place for discussing the stereotype image of the Jews as a state within a state. Is it valid? How was it used? Is it still used?

FOUR
Hitler's Anti-Semitism

This chapter illustrates the ultimate denial of emancipation which was so crucial to the European Jewish community. The writings and speeches illustrate the beginnings of a philosophy which denied the world order which had evolved and had declared human rights as essential to the new social order.

Themes

1. The explicit denial of emancipation
2. The emergence of racial theory and planning
3. The unequivocal indictment of the Jew as an alien "racial" group
4. The sources of the plan to destroy the Jewish people

Discussion

1. What is the significance of calling Jews a race?
2. Does an overall philosophy give greater legitimacy to an immoral plan?
3. Trace the various categories of charges leveled against the Jews. Are there any new categories in this list?

FIVE
Nazi Legislation

This chapter demonstrates how a legal system can be used to validate immoral acts through legislation. It raises the question of morality in the legislative process which has become so relevant recently.

Theme

The legitimization of hate through the legal system

Discussion and Activity

1. Note and discuss the specific laws in terms of anti-Semitic charges read in other documents.
2. What effect does the framing of laws have on a populace?
3. Is it proper to question the morality of the law of the land? If so, what action can be taken?
4. Find illustrations in American history of moral challenges to bona fide legislation.
5. Divide the class into small groups. Assign each group one law to discuss and analyze for its implications. (A good resource for translations of Nazi anti-Semitic legislation is Chapter Two of *A Holocaust Reader* by Lucy S. Dawidowicz published by Behrman House, available in paperback.)

SIX
Unwanted!

This chapter illustrates how innocent men and women became victims of powerful world forces which caused them to abandon morality for "practicality."

Themes

1. The conflict between knowing what is right and being able to act based on information
2. The self-interest of nations
3. The possibility of negative effects when action is half-hearted and weak

Discussion

1. What actions can individual leaders take in the face of threatening national goals and interests?
2. Could Roosevelt have affected the course of the Nazi plan?
3. Did this aborted attempt really help Nazi propaganda?
4. Are there other such incidents in recent times?

SEVEN

Murder

This chapter shows how the "Final Solution" and the use of technology may have been the refinement of a still uncertain plan. The offhanded reporting gives further insight into the total acceptance of horror by educated and responsible people.

Themes

1. The acceptance of murder as a function of state policy
2. The willingness to allow murder to take place
3. The reality of horror

Discussion

1. How could responsible human beings become parties to planned genocide?
2. Do recent events indicate similar public acceptance of immoral acts sanctioned by a government?

EIGHT

Isolation

The "Final Solution" was still being formulated. This section examines the process of isolating the Jewish community, and the reaction of the Jewish community to this process.

Themes

1. The concept of physical isolation, and the privations suffered by its Jewish victims
2. Jewish responses to isolation
3. The activities of both Nazis and Jews

Discussion

1. What was the concept of "isolation"?
2. What were the reactions of the Jews?
3. Are there parallels to this action anywhere in history? (You may wish to consider the internment of Japanese Americans during World War II.)

NINE

The Roundup

Alexander Donat's description of how the Jews were misled by the resettlement myth, caught unaware by the methodology of the German officials, and—in some cases—even forced to turn against one another, creates vividly a brutal and unacceptable reality. From the German point of view the success of the roundup was essential to the carrying out of the "Final Solution." But even at this stage it was the demoralization of the Jews which made possible the implementation of the Nazi horror.

Themes

1. The resettlement myth—why the Jews were anxious to believe it

2. The brutalization of the Jews
3. The centrality of the roundup to the German purpose

Discussion

1. How and why did the Jews submit to the roundup?
2. How was it possible for the Germans to turn brother against brother?
3. Compare and contrast the roundup of the Jews to the roundup of blacks in Africa by their fellow blacks during the years of the slave trade.

TEN

Systematic Destruction

The use of modern technology to destroy a civilian population was a new aspect of horror never before employed. This added dimension to the "Final Solution" raises the question of morality in technological society.

Themes

1. Technology as a neutral force
2. The implications of the immoral use of modern technology

Discussion and Activity

1. What is the proper use of technology?
2. Collect pictures, essays, writings about the proper and improper uses of technology.
3. Should there be worldwide control of science and technology?
4. Are there any attempts to control technology today?

ELEVEN
Jewish Resistance

This chapter should serve to dispel the impression that resistance was not part of the Jewish response. There were many resisters and courageous acts of resistance in the face of overwhelming power.

Themes

1. The attempt to inform the world of Nazi horror and stimulate action
2. The recognition by the Jews of the reality of their situation
3. The resisters' willingness to die

Discussion

1. Why were the resisters willing to die?
2. How well did they understand their situation?
3. What is the difference from, or similarity to, Masada?

TWELVE
War Trials

The world's recognition of the horror of the Holocaust came late, and its willingness to deal with it as a moral world issue, and not as just another incident in human history, can even now be called into question.

Themes

1. The recognition of the Nuremberg Trials by the United States as a moral issue
2. The new concept of "crimes against humanity"

3. The difference between personal involvement as obedience to the state and the individual's responsibility to his or her conscience

Discussion and Activity

1. What is a "crime against humanity"?
2. How do these trials compare with the Calley trial?
3. When must immoral demands of the state be resisted?
4. What is the value, if any, of public trials?
5. This unit lends itself to sociodramatic role-playing, and could be the basis of an interesting class presentation.

THIRTEEN
Feelings

Portrayals of the tragedy and drama of the Holocaust often omit personal emotions. This chapter is a paean of praise to the nobility of spirit exhibited by the victims and survivors of the Holocaust.

Themes

1. The varieties of emotions possible under dire circumstances
2. The brutal reality of good people in a bad world

Discussion and Activity

1. Why did people write poetry? Is that unusual? Are there other illustrations of similar poems?
2. Discuss the activities of the various groups and individuals who saved Jews. You might want to write to the various survivor organizations and get information on these individuals and groups.

CLARENCE L. AND ESTELLE S. MEYERS LIBRARY
Reform Congregation Keneseth Israel
Elkins Park, Pa. 19117

940.5
Z6a
C.2   Zisenwine, David W., ed.
        Anti-Semitism in Europe.

DATE DUE			

Meyers Library

Reform Congregation Keneseth Israel

Elkins Park, PA 19117